In **Kennedy Music**, Ray is a charismatic, hot-swing trumpet player who comes to Maplewood and opens a music school and store at the height of the Great Depression. Mae is a demure, starstruck beauty 20 years his junior. Together they work to raise a family and keep their small business afloat as the world -- and the music industry -- changes around them. This true story, vividly told by their daughter Wanda Kennedy Kuntz, spans over four decades in which shellac records eventually evolved into cassette tapes, and sweet big band jazz gave way to rock 'n' roll. It recalls an era when a music store could serve as the heart for an entire town, and when a family reached beyond a simple brick and mortar store to make their mark on the world around them.

"For nearly half a century, a Maplewood business provided to the community what no community should be without — joyful sounds of people singing, dancing and playing musical instruments.

Wanda Kennedy Kuntz, daughter of Ray and Mae Kennedy, has created an attention-grabbing historical novel with appeal far beyond Maplewood. I highly recommend this wonderful telling of a colorful, truly American story."
— *Doug Houser, Maplewood historian*

*Born and raised in Maplewood, MO, Wanda Kennedy Kuntz is a Maplewood-Richmond Heights alumnae. She received a Master's Degree in Music Performance from Webster University. She is a professional musician, music director and piano instructor.*

**Many thanks to:**

Mom and Dad,
I love you

~ ~ ~

Uncle Tom,
for capturing our history with your camera

~ ~ ~

Hazel, Chuck and Peggy C, and brothers Tom and Ray,
for your love, support and recollections

~ ~ ~

Bill, Kathy, Kristy, Brian and Peggy K,
for your patience and input

~ ~ ~

Alice,
for your inspirational granddaughter cuteness

~ ~ ~

Maplewood,
my hometown

Kennedy Music

An Historical Novel
based on the Kennedy Family

Maplewood, MO

Wanda Kennedy Kuntz

ISBN: 978-1-4951-1840-1 (Print Version)
ISBN: 978-1-4951-1841-8 (E-Book Version)

Printed in the United States of America

# INTRODUCTION

A few years back, I received a phone call from a woman who had recently moved into my childhood home on Vine Street in Maplewood. She wanted to know if I was "part of the family who used to own Kennedy Music Store in Maplewood." I told her my birth name indeed is Kennedy, and when she graciously allowed me to tour my childhood home again, my mind was flooded with memories.

Perhaps this trip to Vine Street was the impetus that brought me back into my past to discover where the music came from. After some research, I have found that the thread of music is in my family tree as far back as the pictures and newspaper clippings in my closet. It has been my great joy to discover at least a segment of that thread. On my mother's side of the family, I have been told there was a violin maker, who also worked for the railroad. A picture of a string trio, hanging in my brother's home studio, was a mystery to all of us until we discovered, comparing the faces in the photo to other old photos stashed away, the three performers were our dad's grandfather and two of his brothers. My mother never had a music lesson in her life but her voice filled our home with the songs of every Broadway musical of her day. My dad was a big band leader and trumpet player, and my uncle and his wife loved to dance. Down through the present day, that thread of music can be found, not only in Wanda, Ray and Tom, but in our children. It reaches into the heart of one of my nieces, who recently declared to her father, Ray, "you will always be my piano teacher."

My siblings and I, and related cousins, share a distinct event and a real place that helped shape all of us -- Kennedy Music Store in Maplewood, Missouri. My two brothers and I, in many ways, grew into the people we are today, because of our parents' music store. We all three share the unusual gift of perfect pitch, and the privilege and pleasure of working solely as professional musicians throughout our lives. We share more than just the memory of a long-ago family business. It is still a "place" that reminds us of who we are on a daily basis. It still serves as a playground for musical exploration and future dreams. It was the birthplace of lifetime friendships with many.  It's also a place that we recall -- with future generations of Kennedys at every family gathering -- that amuses and inspires us.  This story, based upon our family's music store, and our hometown of Maplewood, Missouri, is written to inspire you to see a "thread" inside you -- that helps you recollect, and reconnect to, a place and time that helped you find yourself, and the person you always knew you could be.

This book is for future Kennedys -- future generations of our family -- as well as for music makers and music lovers everywhere.

# CHAPTER 1
## Embraceable You *(George and Ira Gershwin)*

### 1945

18-year-old Edith Mae Heimberger would take the streetcar to meet him. The day had not turned out as she had expected, so this trip she had planned had now become a bit more complicated. That temper of hers had gotten the better of her, and she hadn't really had enough time to figure out what to do about it. The change in her pocketbook would just make the 5-cent streetcar fare. But the line at the Olive Street stop was long -- she hoped she could make it to her destination early enough. Her blonde locks, carefully lacquered into shape prior to her leaving work, were lifted up by a sudden gust of wind.

*"Terrific* -- the headscarf he liked so much at the party -- I must have left it at work. My hair's gonna be a mess." A nice gentleman offered her his seat as she boarded the #53 streetcar. Good thing -- this trip might take awhile. The streetcar wound its way slowly around its curves at Olive

and Washington streets in downtown St. Louis, and then toddled its way west along Chouteau. Then at Manchester it was headed more southwest — and fairly far away from any landmarks Mae knew. Finally, the #53 halted at the City Limits loop at the intersection of Manchester and Yale.

Mae had a choice, at this point, to get off and walk a bit, to ride a little farther up Manchester, to ride all the way to the Maplewood loop at Sutton just past her destination — or to forget the whole idea and just stay on the streetcar as it wound its way back. She decided that last choice just wasn't an option for her.

The 1945 Christmas rush in Maplewood was in full swing. Well beyond the loop full of streetcars, busses and cars, Mae could see there was lots of hustle and bustle. She decided to get off and walk a bit — and to think about things. As soon as her high-heeled pumps touched the pavement, she quickly made her way through the crowds to the sidewalk.

She took a moment to admire the ornate roofs and windows of the Maplewood shops -- each building and facade a unique shape and design. There was a bit of a small-town atmosphere — more trees and shrubs than she was used to in the more urban South City -- but there was nothing small-townish in what Maplewood had to offer. The storefronts were impeccably designed and the windows beautifully framed with tinsel, snowflakes and colorful lights. Already dark outside! The cold was penetrating. Now, just where was that music store? He had said it was near the 7300 block of Manchester Avenue, which was a bit west of the Maplewood "picture show" which she could see straight ahead of her, and the spacious Brownsom Hotel, which loomed immediately on her left. That's where she had heard him play that night.

Short blocks to the music store, she hoped! Mae began her trek at the curb of the 7100 block and headed west past Loop Drugs. Along the 7200 block she saw McCoy's Restaurant across Manchester. She walked past Ladd Brothers Shell Station, the Velvet Freeze, and then further up, the butcher's shop. As she made her way past the butcher shop, she flinched when she realized the butcher was actually in the alley behind the shop, slaughtering a fresh chicken for someone's dinner!  She stood still.

"I hope that mother of his has gone home for the evening."

Louise Kennedy had been no easy woman to talk to, especially when it came to the subject of her unattached son, Ray.  Why had Louise attended the dance that Saturday evening?  She appeared a bit too prim and proper even to dance a waltz, let alone any of the new dances.

Mae felt the cold deep in her bones and she realized she had to keep moving.  Her high heels moved again briskly  — she kept heading west.  Across the street on the south side she spied Empire Supply, the Stertzing Florist building,  and the Toll House restaurant. By now she was starving.

So just why had Louise been so hard to talk to that night?  Yes, of course everyone realized there was an age difference between them (Ray was 20 years older than Mae), but that just didn't seem to matter to either of them.  Younger men had always been a bore to her anyway.  So why was Louise so blatantly concerned about it when Ray introduced them?  Mae didn't usually waste much time deciding what she wanted — and Ray's mother's opinions were not going to get the better of *her*.

As she continued west along Manchester she noticed EJ's pharmacy and Mary George Bridal Shop on the south side of  the street a little up ahead.   Since she was seeing a few 7300 addresses, she knew she was getting close.  She turned her eyes toward the right — there it was.

He had said it was located in a rather large building on the northeast corner of Manchester and Oakview Terrace — the old Maplewood Bank Building. She walked past the various storefronts within the bank building. There was Herman's Toggery, Globe Shoe Repair, and then she saw the entrance door to Kennedy Music and Hobby Shop. She also noticed Johnny Ray's Beauty Shop -- how she wished she had time and money to stop in for a quick style.

Mae wondered again why she had been so excited to make this streetcar trip. She took a moment to reconsider — then took one glove off and smoothed her wind-blown hair. She turned and stepped inside the music shop, and demurely approached the man behind the cash register. "Excuse me, sir -- do you happen to have that wonderful recording — *Sunrise Serenade* by Frankie Carle?"

Ray immediately recognized that soft, alluring voice — something about the way she spoke already felt familiar. He looked up from the register into her blue eyes -- what a knockout. "I think we can set you up with a record or two. Wanna get a bite to eat first?"

"Sure."

"Lots of places to eat around here!  Mom's gone home already, or I would have taken you back to say hello.  I had a late lunch today, but a sandwich sounds good.  Hey Dale -- do you think you can handle things while I take Mae out for a bite?"

"Yes, Mr. Kennedy . . . but what about that customer who had the guitar in will-call?"

"Oh, I doubt Larry will be back in tonight.  We'll probably see him in here next week sometime."

"Did you leave a name tag on the case..."

Ray was too taken with Mae to respond. "Come on, Mae -- I'll show you the town."

Her mom had brought the new coat home for her the night before, and she was grateful -- this was definitely the night to wear it.

"Sorry I'm so late getting here.  It was a long day at work, and I didn't realize the streetcar ride out here was so long.  And then I hopped off the streetcar a little too soon since I was trying to find my way …"

"So you didn't take the streetcar the other night to the Brownsom?"

"No — we drove."

The couple walked west, passing Western Auto, Citizen's Bank, Goldes Department Store, and Martyn's —The Shop for Women. Across Manchester was F. W. Woolworth's, and by this time Mae's feet were numb from the cold. She was more than ready to stop. "We have a Woolworth's near where I live -- could we cross here and take a look?"

"Sure -- but let's go to the Maplewood Cafe on Sutton, next to the bowling alley. If I had a little more time before that last trumpet student, I'd take you for a more relaxed meal at the Tollhouse, but I hope this works out okay for you tonight."

They were seated by Vi, the owner, and Ray placed the order. Then he grabbed Mae's hands and rubbed them — they were freezing.

"Happy birthday, by the way," she said.

Ray smiled. "Aw — you remembered!" He gazed into her admiringly. "So d'ya mind my calling you Geranium?"

"Why Geranium?"

"Oh, I've always thought geraniums were beautiful."

She thought a moment ... "D'ya mind my calling you Heathcliff?"

He hesitated. "Heathcliff, like from... let's see..."

"Wuthering Heights, silly."

"Right ... I was gonna say that. Sure, why not? By the way, I enjoyed the dance last weekend. I normally don't dance at those parties

-- especially during a trumpet job -- and I normally don't dance as much as you and I did under the best of circumstances. Lots of fun! Evelyn was a good sport about it."

"You're talking about the girl who sang ..."

"Yeah -- nice voice, don't you think? Yep -- I don't think she minded that we were dancing, uh…" Ray began to stumble over his words as he realized he'd put his foot in his mouth.

"Oh, really," Mae interjected playfully. "So *Evelyn* was okay with you and me ..."

Ray's eyes twinkled as he laughed. "Now don't get your nose all bent out of shape. People still seem to think Evelyn and I are an item, but the day I laid eyes on you, *I* knew Evelyn was history."

"So he likes me," Mae thought to herself. Suddenly the diner felt much warmer and relaxed. Not to mention, the grilled Velveeta cheese sandwich and dill pickle spear tasted surprisingly good.

"How often do the New Yorkers play? That's the name of your orchestra, right?"

"Yep — that's the orchestra you heard. Oh, usually a couple of nights a week. Sometimes during the summer we've played at the Meramec Highlands, and we have played for the Veiled Prophet Ball. Along with the Brownsom ballroom, we've been also playing the dances down at 7314 Manchester on Wednesday evenings. My other orchestra, the Rhythm Boys, sometimes gets together down at Concordia Turner Hall at 13th and Arsenal. You should sing with us somctime."

"Are you kidding?" Secretly she wished she could get up the nerve to perform. Memories took her back to a tap dance studio in Soulard. She and her mom had heard the tapping feet on their way home, and Mae had asked, "Do you think I could take dance lessons there someday,

Mom?" Her mother bruskly r e p l i e d , "Honey, it's enough I'm able to keep a roof over our head." But a girl could dream, couldn't she?

Ray had already finished his plate. His voice brought her back to the present. "What did you think of the piano player? I love it when I can get Art Crimmons to tickle the ivories with the band. Great guy. He really draws the dance crowds."

Mae twirled and played with her paper straw flirtatiously. "So how long have you had the business?"

"Tom and Mary opened the music store ... well, about 5 years ago now. The music and dance studios were started sooner than that. Mom and Dad helped us get things up and running -- I guess that was 1934. Mom teaches piano, I teach some instruments and dancing, and Tom and Mary teach ballroom dance classes. We've built it up from there — we employ about 10 teachers now. You haven't seen the instrumental and dance studios above the record store yet, have you? We even have an auditorium or two with a stage — my dad and brother did quite a bit of carpentry work. I'll have to take you up there."

Mae thought about 1934 for a moment. He had said the music studios had opened In 1934. In 1934 she was only 7 years old!

Ray continued. "I told Tom that if he and Mary wanted us to open a store, they'd have to do it. Mother and I had plenty to do running the school upstairs."

Ray shared with Mae a memory of the very first music store sale -- the man needing a record needle. Mary, still new to the business, was on her own that evening.

"'Is this the best record needle available?' the gentleman had asked Mary. She replied, 'Yes, sir.' And Mary wasn't lying. It was literally the *only* record needle we had in stock that day. The man bought it!"

Mae laughed. "Mary sure knew how to think on her feet. You introduced me to your mother the other night. I'm just curious — isn't her name Louise? She just wouldn't stop raving about you and your brother. What are her responsibilities? How many hours is she able to work?"

Ray looked a bit pensive. "Louise is a strong woman," he continued. "She has had to be, especially since our dad's passing. She keeps the books and the inventory - and keeps Tom, me and the teachers on our toes."

"I wish Victor had been as understanding as…what's her name… Evelyn…the other night. He was all bent out of shape today."

"So that's the name of the guy that was at the Brownsom that night. He's the same guy you work with at S. G. Adams downtown? He looked like trouble."

"I've always loved stationery stores. I love working at S. G. Adams." She decided not to tell him -- not just yet anyway. "Besides -- I would have never heard of Ray Kennedy, and the Brownsom Hotel in Maplewood, if it hadn't been for Victor. He's a real music lover."

"Well, *if* you're interested at some point, we sure could use a sheet music clerk in the store downstairs. Just seems like everyone who walks in these days is asking for the words and music to *Rum and Coca Cola*. Tom is taking photography more and more seriously, and the music store is becoming quite a lot to handle."

"Well I don't know about that...but thanks for the offer."

"Hey -- wanna go have some fun?" After Mae finished her last bite of food, Ray playfully grabbed Mae's hand and they took off briskly back to the music store to check in with Dale.

"Mr. Kennedy," Dale quipped as they walked in, "Larry from the shoe store WAS back in while you we're gone. He brought in his last payment, and he really wants to pick up the guitar tonight but you didn't tag it..."

"Aw now don't worry --I'll walk it down to him in a bit. Come on, Mae — I've got something to show you."

"Hold on, big brother. Aren't you going to introduce us?" Ray suddenly noticed his brother, Tom, and his wife, Mary, turning around to face him from the record stacks. Tom was holding their 3-year-old son, and Mary was holding their newborn daughter.

"Well hey there, Tom and Mary! Didn't see you standing there. I'd like you to meet...Geranium. Just kidding." He looked into her eyes and gently asked, "What should we call you, seriously?"

"Oh, Mae is fine."

"Good to meet you, Mae," said Mary.

"And I'd say you're pretty enough to be a geranium." Tom leaned over and kissed Mae on the cheek. "Ray, Mary and I can help mind the store during your trumpet lesson."

"Thanks, Tom." Ray gently whisked Mae outside again, and around to the music school entrance. She tried to keep up with his wide strides up the stairway. At the top of the steps he turned her toward the new *Voice-O-Matic* recording booth. The outside of the booth said, "Record your voice -- hear yourself as others hear you." Ray and Tom were always interested in the latest technology.

Mae stopped in her tracks. "No, Ray -- I won't know what to say. I'll get tongue-tied. This is silly ..."

Before she could stop him, Ray blocked her exit of the booth, grabbed the tokens out of his pocket, dropped them into the slot, and then in a moment he quietly pointed to the lit sign, *Studio in operation. Wait for light below.* She watched as the six-inch record disc appeared, and dropped into place. Ray gently placed his hands on her shoulders from behind just to keep her still as she began to squirm and fidget a bit. "Just sing something you know -- you have a beautiful voice." *Ready* -- a light came on, and as the needle flipped over ready to cut the vinyl she suddenly fell speechless. Good thing Ray was never at a loss for words!

"Come on, Mae -- now just tell me what you think of this new-fangled thing..."

"Great...." was all she could manage to spit out.

"Now Mae ... uh ... how do you like the Christmas lights in Maplewood?"

No answer.

"And the Christmas lights downtown?"

"Sure…" She felt really silly.

"Yeah, and … Maizey … are you planning to meet me at the dance club after Christmas? Maybe we should make it a date to ring in the new year together."

"Oh … Ray!" Now she was embarrassed.

"You're a really good dancer, Mae -- lets go dancing again, okay?"

"Okay…" Mae glanced up at the lighted message -- *35 seconds to go* -- She was in agony.

"What d'ya want for Christmas, Mae?"

"Uh … my two front teeth?"

Her remark broke the ice. Ray chuckled loudly in his usual way. "Good one! Good one! Now, we're almost done. Ya know, Mom, Tom and I could sure use your help at the music store, and I know you can sing the hits better than my brother Tom. You seem to know the words to all the new songs."

A little more time to fill. *10 seconds to go…*

Mae felt warm inside. She had made Ray laugh. And the way she scarfed down that grilled cheese at Maplewood Cafe -- she couldn't remember the last time she had such an appetite. As of today she needed a new job -- and her pride told her she couldn't go groveling back to S. G. Adams. Not to that sorry excuse of a supervisor. But Maplewood was a long way down the streetcar line, and her 12-year-old sister would have to be alone a little longer in the evenings while their mom worked — that is, *IF* she took Ray up on the offer.

"What do you think, Mae? D'ya like it here?" He lightly brushed back her blonde hair. Did he just read her mind?

*Stop -- recording is complete.* The needle lifted, adjusted and then replayed the record back to them. That same gentle hand that had held her hand so tightly up the music store stairs, came to rest lightly on her shoulder while they listened to the playback in silence. Her blue eyes and his blue eyes met intently. Then, as the record dropped into the tray — like magic, her mind was made up. Ray reached down, lifted the dispenser window to retrieve the record and mailing sleeve, and gently pressed the finished product into her hand. She kept a hold of his fingers. They kissed.

"We open at 9:30 am day after Christmas. See you then -- bright and early?"

# CHAPTER 2
## Oh Mein Papa *(Paul Burkhard)*

### 1946

Mae felt a mixture of emotions as she stepped toward the front door of 2901a Vincent Avenue. The weeks and months had flown by — never before in her life had she felt so free and happy. But earlier that day, when she received the phone call, she knew from Hazel's tone she needed to be with her sister and family. She rang the doorbell. Her mother, Bertha, came downstairs and opened the door. Mae hugged her mom as they made their way up to the apartment.

"Honey, thank you for stopping by this evening. Now just how long has it been since we've seen you? I'm so glad you could get away from the music store for a bit tonight. Come on in."

As they entered the apartment, Mae saw the familiar figure behind her mother — someone she had not seen for a very, very long time.

"Edith Mae — good to see you."

"Hi, Dad." There was a palpable tension that made the thought of embracing one another seem just too awkward.

Already seated at the kitchen table was her younger brother, Joe — his body slouched, legs spread across the floor and his arms folded across his chest. After a hint of a nod toward his older sister as she entered, he immediately looked back down again. Hazel, the youngest of the three, was adding a little pepper to the beef gravy. She appeared very stiff and upset.

"Hi, Mae." Hazel certainly didn't seem like her chipper self.

"Here — let me help you, Hazel." Mae was hoping to get a clue of what was going on.

Hazel replied quickly, "No, no. I'm doing just fine, Mae. Take your coat off — dinner is about ready."

Bertha walked hand in hand with her ex-husband John into the living room. Mae wasn't sure what to make of this. The three of them sat down, and after feeling the weight of a long silence, Bertha spoke.

"Mae, tell your dad all about your new job."

Mae wasn't in the mood for small talk, but went along with it. "Okay — I'm working at a music store. It's in Maplewood."

"Never heard of Maplewood," her dad commented.

"It's a little west of St. Louis City, Dad — but not too far away from here on the streetcar."

"It's far enough, Mae," Bertha jumped in, jovially. "I never see you."

"Mom, you should come out tomorrow — it's Saturday. We're preparing for another dance recital, and we're finishing the costumes."

Hazel stepped in to the living room. "Are you still wanting my help on  the costumes, Mae?"

Bertha stopped Hazel. "Hazel, you know you're doing that bundling job on Saturdays. You know it was hard for me to get that job for you — lots of girls wanted it."

"At least you don't have to lace moccasins, Hazel," Joe's tone was sarcastic, in an effort to get his little sister to lighten up. Joe was recalling a time when their mother found extra income at a moccasin factory. She would bring the moccasin pieces home, and have the kids lace them up in the evenings.

"You know, Mae, *you* could have had that bundling job," Bertha said. "The work is good, now that the war is over and people are buying again. If you decide to move back home…"

Hazel overheard her mom's statement. "I personally think Mae was smart to get out of here when she did. Dinner's ready." She glared at her father and turned back around toward the kitchen.

"Hazel, stop it," Joe, in a muffled voice, was trying to ward off an argument between Hazel and her parents, which Hazel had seemed determined to start all afternoon. "Dad's just trying to be a dad."

"Young lady, I won't allow you to speak that way to your mother," John said with an authority Hazel didn't think he had earned. Joe could tell Hazel was about to lose it.

She bit her lip and brought the serving bowls to the table. The family made the sign of the cross before filling their plates.

At long last, Bertha was ready to share what was on her mind. "Kids, we have a couple of important announcements to make. First of all, Mae and Hazel, your brother Joe has just signed up with the United States Army."

A long silence ensued. Mae gathered up her courage to ask. "Joe, I thought your job with the railroad was a good one."

"Well, yes and no, Mae," Bertha answered for her son. "Joe has a bit more time on his hands than he needs. The army will help instill some discipline — and it will give him a chance to travel — right, John?"

"Travel?" Mae asked.

"Yep. I'll most likely be going to Austria." Joe spoke without much enthusiasm.

"But the war …."

"*Occupied* Germany, Hazel," John said. The war is over. You know that." He paused for a bite of potatoes. "This will be good for your brother. He's not a child anymore, and he needs to find a good trade. Your mother and I wanted him to get on at Mississippi Glass as a glass cutter apprentice, since I've worked there for so long, but they don't have any openings right now. The army will help him develop a skill."

Mae leaned in toward her young brother. "Joe, is this what you want…"

John answered abruptly. "Hell, Mae — what kid at the age of 16 knows what he wants to do with his life?" Bertha looked worried — she reached over and squeezed John's hand. After noting her concern, John took a breath, calmed himself and continued. "Joe knows deep down this is what's best for him. We've had some good talks about it, haven't we, Son?"

"And now the other bit of news," suddenly Bertha was bubbling over with enthusiasm. Her eyes teared up a bit as she looked around at everyone. "Your father and I — well kids — I don't really know the best way to break the news, so I'll just say it — we're getting married again."

Immediately Hazel burst into tears and ran from the table. Joe just rolled his eyes and, not wanting to make more waves, continued to eat. Mae excused herself and followed Hazel up to her bedroom. Bertha called out as Mae approached the upstairs stairway. "Honey, she's been grumpy all evening. Come back and eat — Hazel will be fine."

The two sisters climbed up into Hazel's bed. "Mae, for the past few weeks I knew something was going on. I really can't take it. I don't know the man. Remember — just a couple of years ago she took him to court for child support, and lost. How come now, after all these years, they're suddenly back together and getting along so great?"

Hazel blew her nose and tried to stop her crying. Mae held her close.

Hazel eventually continued. "You always told me Mom was pregnant with me when they split up. He's been married to someone else all this time. And now, I guess that marriage must be over, since Mom's talking about the three of us leaving South St. Louis and moving up somewhere north — a street called John Avenue. She's talking about me finishing my schooling up there! I won't know anybody!"

Mae interjected. "I could understand it if you were younger, Hazel, when Mom was needing someone to watch you all the time while she was working. You hated the boarding school in Ironton when you were in first grade, but we all understood Mom had to do it."

"I know! I can take care of myself now. And if I have to go with them all the way up there, I'll be even farther away from you — and now Joe…" She grabbed her pillow and the tears flowed again.

"But that's just it, Hazel. Mom may really be happier now with Dad around, and we'd all like that. I promise I'll talk with her. We'll work out something. Now let's go back downstairs."

"No, Mae — you go. I really do want Mom to be happy, but I've honestly had all I can take for now."

Mae returned downstairs, and she finished eating in silence. John, Bertha and Joe had moved back into the living room, and were admiring magazine pictures of the Austrian Alps, mountainside chalets and beautiful Alpine ladies in colorful dirndl dresses.

"Ready for cake and coffee, Mae?" Bertha asked.

Mae walked into the living room and picked up her clutch purse. "I'm sorry, Mom — I really don't have time for dessert tonight — I need to head back. Thank you, though."

Everyone but Hazel walked with Mae toward the front door. John leaned toward his older daughter and said, "Edith Mae, you'll need to introduce us — I believe your mother said Ray is a trumpet player. Next time, I want you to bring him along so I can meet him. And your mother mentioned your living arrangements — something about Ray's mother's apartment?"

Mae hesitated before responding to her dad.

Bertha had already met Ray, and had enjoyed several visits with him. He brought his trumpet along, and Bertha loved the opportunity to bring out her banjo. The two of them, very close in age, shared a quick wit and a gift for gab. Bertha knew how happy Mae was with Ray, and didn't press the issue of trying to control Mae's whereabouts. Mae had become her own person, making her own choices and decisions, and intended to remain that way.

"Ray's mother has given me the sofa in her apartment above the store. You know, Dad, it might be easier for you to come meet Ray in Maplewood. Running a business takes a lot of hours, and when he isn't working at the store he's performing with his orchestra."

Bertha handed Mae a bag. "Here, Honey — take the rest of the cake home for Ray and his mother."

Joe walked her downstairs. "Take care, Sis."

Mae was overcome with love and concern toward her younger brother. She wept as they embraced at the bottom of the stairs. The responsibility of watching out for two younger siblings had fallen to Mae when she was young herself, and had continued until very recently. Their mother had worked very long days at dress factories throughout their childhood. So, hopefully their dad being back in the picture again, as strange as it seemed now, was for the best. Maybe — just maybe — Mom could be at home and not work as much.

But this news about Joe — he was just too young to be doing this — he was actually under the legal age to join the army. Either Bertha or John was pulling strings to get him in. After all she had done to keep the three kids under her roof, how could Mom possibly agree to this?

"So Joe, when do you think you'll be leaving the country?"

He lit up a cigarette as they walked outside. "I won't be leaving at least until after basic training." He wanted to reassure his big sister, even though he himself wasn't convinced he wanted to go. "Listen — I'll be okay. It isn't wartime. Hell — I might find some of our ancestors over there, if there are any left. Dad told me his folks fled Europe, took the boat to Canada, and then made their way down to St. Louis." He took another draw on his cigarette. "I'll bring some stationery so I can write all of you."

"Joe, I guess if you're okay with enlisting I'm okay with it. I'll look after Hazel. I'll talk with Ray tomorrow — there might be a bus that could bring Hazel into Maplewood once a week or so for music lessons. That would give her and me a chance to spend more time together. I know you've been wanting to talk to Dad for years. For whatever reason the two of them are wanting you to enlist, I'm glad you've been able to spend some time with Dad again." They hugged again. "Just be careful, little brother."

"How long before the streetcar comes?"

"Not long. You go ahead back in — maybe you and Hazel can talk a bit."

As the door closed behind her, Mae paused and looked around.

Her family now lived about a mile from St. John Nepomuk and the old parish school which she had attended. It was when she was 5 or 6 that her tearful mother, her brother Joe and she quickly packed up and moved out, finding an apartment in the Nepomuk parish. As the oldest child, Mae decided she'd help her mother keep a roof over their heads.

Still very small, one errand she enjoyed was buying milk at the corner grocery. Trudging through several inches of winter snow along the South City sidewalks, she'd make a game of sinking the heavy milk

22

jug into the snow, heaving it back up, and then jumping with both feet into the hole it made — a kind of hop scotch.

Mae remembered her school chores, which included arriving early to dust and arrange the pews before morning Mass. She also remembered the day she got caught chewing gum in class, and feeling humiliated when the teacher made her chew in front of everyone. She remembered the day she brought her bologna sandwich to school, and being reminded by her teacher not to eat it because it was a Friday. "Silly rules," her mother told her later. "Don't worry your little head about them."

She remembered waking up one night and overhearing her mother's sister, Aunt Dell, talking downstairs with her mother. John had gotten married again. He was living on Delmar with his new wife. Young Mae tried to make sense of this. Had her mom made a mistake leaving her dad? Did Dad even remember his children existed?

Would the Church continue to help them, even when Mae forgot the rules and ate meat on Fridays? The Mother Superior seemed nice — providing a beautiful dress for her on the occasion of her First Communion. But Mae also heard stories of families torn apart, and orphanages for children of parents who couldn't buy food or pay their rent on time.

As a child Mae escaped from her worries with movies at Lowe's Theatre, and books at the City Library on Lafayette Street. There were occasional bus trips to Bertha's parents in Ironton — and months living with her mother's mother for reasons she didn't understand.

Into her young teen years, she would pack Joe and Hazel's school lunches, and keep the South City apartment so clean that she made them take their shoes off before entering. Keeping things in order, as the family moved from one flat to another throughout the brutal 1930's, was something Mae could do — a way she could maintain some sense of control despite the disappointment and turmoil around her.

Mae took a deep breath. She'd recently grown to love this time in the evening — sitting with Ray somewhere outside — when the sun had not quite set, as her cares slipped further and further away, into an ever-deepening sky of azure blue. Ray always seemed so relaxed and calm. Bittersweet childhood memories would always remain with her, but somehow, working in Maplewood, they didn't seem as threatening anymore.

She realized it was much later now. She'd better get home. She headed over just in time for the next streetcar, and with a smile on her lips she stepped up onto the platform, greeted the streetcar operator, dropped the nickel into the slot, and enjoyed the ride back into her new life.

~ ~ ~ ~ ~ ~ ~ ~ ~ ~ ~ ~ ~ ~ ~ ~ ~

Saturday mornings were noisy at Kennedy School of Music and Dance. At the back end of the upstairs hallway the tap dance instructor called out, "Step, shuffle, ball-change! Step, shuffle, ball-change! Brush...brush..." and the tap shoes tapped away in varying degrees of rhythmic skill. The next studio, much smaller in size, held a young drum student and his snare drum, trying out his paradiddles, flams and ratamacues. As Mae made her way down the hallway she peered in to see the guitar class tuning up — one of these days she was determined to try out an instrument or two. She found the mothers in yet another small studio, gathering to complete the finishing work on the costumes, while their future stars rehearsed. Louise was there, and so was Mary, Tom's wife — along with their toddler daughter, Peggy.

"Mary," said Louise, "I ran into Ray on my way in. He's planning to take Chuckie with him to the schools this afternoon. As you know, Chuckie has been asking to go for several weeks now, and Ray thinks he's ready. They're going to Mallinkrodt and Lindenwood over the Fyler bridge."

"That makes me so nervous," Mae said.

"Why?" asked Louise.

"Louise, I just don't know why something isn't done about that Fyler

Avenue bridge. I'm nervous anywhere in a car, but that bridge just terrifies me."

"Oh, Mae — I know what you mean," said Mary. That old, rickety wooden bridge. It's so archaic — I hate that thing. When Tom drives into the city to take pictures, that's the route he always takes. He says it's the closest way to get to the Lindenwood neighborhood."

Another of the ladies overheard, and commented. "I've read about so many fatal accidents along there — it's narrow and has that sharp turn. I close my eyes every time my husband drives us over that bridge."

Mary agreed. "I always tell Tom to slow down there. When cars take the bridge too fast, especially on the downgrade coming into Piccadilly Avenue, so many of them have lost control and fallen off the side."

"That's also about the only way Ray and Tom can visit their cousins over on Ivanhoe," explained Louise. "Mae, have you met Cliff and Woody Brown?"

"Ray told me about them. They own that music store on Ivanhoe, right Louise?"

"That's right, continued Louise. They are fine young men. Woody used to take music lessons here as a teenager, and he and his brother recently opened that little music shop on Ivanhoe. I certainly hope that store proves to be successful." Louise smiled as she thought about her cousin, Walter, the streetcar operator. "Why, every time Woody and Cliff's father, Walter, stops the streetcar at our corner, he rings that bell just for me."

Tom walked in with his camera. "Ready for the pictures?"

"Almost, Tom," Mary replied. "after this class, we'll dress and line up the kids for the newspaper picture. Just have a seat."

"How long have you worked for the newspaper, Tom?" Mae asked.

"When Mary and I first got married, the first gift she gave me was a Brownie Camera — right, honey? That was when we had that little apartment over the Maplewood Theatre. From that point on I was hooked. Every day, when my shift ended at Grand Leader downtown, I would take pictures of everything in sight — parades, buildings, passersby. I began developing my own pictures when I set up a dark room right there in the apartment — that's when the fun really started. Later, when the St. Louis County Observer newspaper was looking for a photo journalist, I showed them some of my work and I was hired."

"I'm not surprised," said Mae. "You do beautiful work."

"It's especially fun taking photos of the recording artists and movie stars when they're in town — and of course, the Kennedy School tap dancers in their beautiful costumes."

"Daddy!" In bounced Chuckie, now four years old, right into Tom's lap.

"Hi, Son! What have you been up to this morning?"

"Daddy — guess what? I'm going with Uncle Ray in the car!"

"Is that right? And then what are you going to do, Chuckie?"

"Well — I'm taking my bugle, the one you and Uncle Ray got me — and then when Uncle Ray says it's time — I stand on a chair — and I wreck the band!"

"Wreck the band — what…"

Ray chuckled as he entered the room just behind his nephew. "He means 'di-rect' the band! Tom, you should see it. In fact, the weather looks good for an outside photo at Lindenwood Elementary School, if you want to come along and take some pictures."

Tom started counting the rolls of film in his camera case. "Okay — let's see how long the tap dance photo takes."

Louise interrupted. "Now boys, you need to talk somewhere else. We've got to finish these costumes."

"Let's go, Ray," said Tom. "Say goodbye, Chuckie." In his piping voice, Chuckie said, "Bye Bye, Gam-ma!" and, after giving Louise, Mary, Aunt Mae and little sister Peggy some "sugar," he left with his dad and uncle.

"Bye bye, little Charles Raymond," Louise affectionately replied as she watched him walk down the hallway.

Mae stopped her sewing for a moment and looked straight ahead. "Those dancers seem to be tapping louder than ever today. Did you feel that?"

The other ladies felt it. They all paused. They heard what seemed to be a series of crackling noises.

Mary broke the silence. "Maybe they're rolling the piano across the dance floor, or something! Anyway — Mae, Chuckie just loves that new bugle. It's the cutest thing — he even takes it to bed with him at night. As long as he doesn't try to play it in the middle of the night…"

They thought the crackling was over — now the sounds seemed closer and closer together, and it felt like the room began to move.

They realized the music and tapping had stopped. This wasn't the dancers after all.

Louise stood up. "I think we'd better leave the building. Sound the fire alarm!"

Suddenly the dance class was in a panic. No time to change their shoes. The tap dance instructor helped them converge and move as quickly as possible down the front stairwell. People toward the back studios found their way to the fire escape.

Ray and Tom stood at ground level to help direct people away from the building. From the outside they could see what had happened — large, jagged cracks had split the mortar between the bricks on the west side of the building. Somehow the old building had shifted. Tom was relieved when Mary made her way out the front door with Peggy in her arms. Mae and Louise weren't far behind.

A crowd of passersby had gathered. Part of the fire escape in the back of the building came loose and caused part of the metal rungs to sway.

Tom looked at Ray. "Is everyone out?"

"I think so … where's Chuckie …"

Tom suddenly took off toward the back of the building, looking for his son. Ray made his way around the other direction. They yelled toward one another as they ran.

"Ray, you don't think Chuckie is still in there…"

"I thought he was still with you, Tom…"

Tom ran inside each store nearby. He found Vera Ray from the beauty shop standing outside. He found the people from Globe Shoe Repair. Maybe Mr. Greenlea from the ice cream store had seen him. One by one the store owners said they had not seen Chuck.

Ray bounded up the steps, back through the studios. He frantically called out Chuck's name. He pulled each door open, praying he'd find him.

Suddenly, he heard something. At end of the long hallway, Ray could see a little figure peering outside the partially open door of the big dance studio. Little Chuck had snuck back into the music school. Uncle Ray just hadn't been listening closely enough. When they had heard the loud noises, Daddy whisked him up in his arms and took him outside. Chuck called out as loudly as he could, "Bring my bugle outside, Uncle Ray!" After all, if he was going to "wreck the band" later, he had to have his shiny, new bugle. But Uncle Ray forgot — so Chuck had to find it. After sneaking back in, the building started to shake, so Chuck hid in the corner of the dance studio. He hoped his family wouldn't forget about him, but he was too frightened to move.

Chuck's Uncle Ray spoke gently as not to scare him. "It's okay, Chuckie. Come to me."

"I'm afraid. Am I in trouble?"

"Chuck, run to me now. Let's get out of here."

Ray was afraid his own weight could cause the compromised second floor to collapse underneath them both. The hallway looked very long and steep to Chuck, but he took off running toward his uncle anyway. When Chuck got close enough, Ray lunged forward and scooped Chuck up into his arms. They both walked down the front steps and safely outside.

"Hooray!" The crowd waiting outside was overjoyed.

The whole family stayed with Tom and Mary at their house on Lohmeyer that night.

"What a day," Ray exclaimed, as he collapsed into a comfy chair at Tom's place. "What a weekend," said Mae.

Mr. Fishman, the landlord, worked with the City of Maplewood to begin a process of renovations, repairing sections of this prime location at the northeast corner of Manchester at Oakview Terrace. A building facelift was long overdue.

*The Maplewood Bank Building, which served as the first location of Kennedy School and Store, along with several other businesses, can be seen in photos as early as 1904. It had several renovations over the years. As late as the 1970's it was occupied by an expanded Western Auto store along with several retail establishments. The actual Maplewood Bank did not remain in the building long; shortly after the 1904 construction, the building's namesake found a new home at the northeast corner of Manchester and Sutton relatively soon after Maplewood was incorporated (later occupied by Pioneer Bank and Trust).*

*The Fyler Avenue Bridge was a wooden structure, originally built in 1887 in Cordova, Alabama. In 1907, the Frisco Railroad transported it here, to span the railroad yards and River Des Peres between the Lindenwood neighborhood of the city and the Ellendale area of Maplewood. In spite of the fact that it was built during the time of horse and buggy traffic, it continued to be a primary route for vehicles of all types between Southwest St. Louis and Maplewood, into the late 1950's. In the early 1960's, it was finally barricaded from motorists when plans were drawn up for the construction of Highway 44. It remained a favorite place for bicyclists and pedestrians to stop and look at the trains and River Des Peres, until finally, in January, 1965, the City of St. Louis demolished it in favor of the Arsenal Bridge.*

# CHAPTER 3

## Sentimental Journey *(Les Brown, Ben Homer, Bud Green)*

### 1947

Kennedy School of Music and Dance, particularly the dance, baton and band instrument classes, continued to grow in reputation throughout the Maplewood and surrounding areas. Although Mr. Fishman had just increased the rent due to necessary renovations of the western side and upper floor of the building, the Kennedys could handle it for now. The School office and most of the studios had moved downstairs for safety reasons. Louise's living quarters upstairs remained intact. Louise continued to keep a close eye on Ray and Mae, as it was obvious they cared deeply for each other. In the evenings Louise would often remind Mae it was "unusual that Ray could be captivated by one woman for so long."

Mae, now 20, would enjoy Sunday brunches with John, Bertha and Hazel at their new address on John Avenue. Because the streetcar and bus routes were a little more complicated from Maplewood to North County, Louise's living room was a place for Mae to lay her head during the week. It was kind of Louise to extend that courtesy to her, but it was also mutually beneficial, since Mae was a big help in the music store.

When Ray was busy weekend evenings playing at area restaurants and dance clubs, Tom and Mary, and their children, enjoyed whiling away the evenings with her, playing cards, or listening to the latest hit records. One such evening, Tom brought over a handful of old photographs for Mae to see.

"Tom, I'm confused," said Mae, as she glanced through them. "When was this picture of Ray taken?"

She passed the photo to Louise. "Oh, this is my brother Jimmy — where'd you find this, Tom?"

"I think Ray must have left these at our place a while back," Tom speculated. "I let him keep all the old pictures in one of the closets at the music school."

"Jimmy's mighty handsome in this one, don't you think, Mae?" Louise lovingly placed the picture in Mae's hand.

"It says 'The Bittick-Benson Orchestra' on the drum set," Mae noticed.

"That's right," Tom interjected. "The Bittick-Benson Orchestra was popular in the 1920's. Jimmy is a very talented and well-liked drummer. He knew just what he wanted to do from a very young age, didn't he, Mom?"

"That's very true," Louise said after a deep sigh.

Tom continued. "Later he somehow made some connections with the Philip Morris agency out in L.A., and the orchestra he built there became a favorite of radio audiences. See — here's a picture of him and Ben Terpin…"

"The old movie star?" asked Mae.

"Yes, said Tom. "His orchestra went on tour to places like the huge Edgewater Beach Hotel in Florida."

Tom laughed, as he handed Mae another picture. "Look at those shoes on Uncle Jimmy — you know, Mae, in the 1920's men wore those stylish spats on their shoes. Here's Jimmy showing off his spats, stepping up on the running board of the limo — quite the dapper fellow."

"Now, this picture's signed by him." Mae tilted the photograph toward the light. "Let's see what it says…'Will always serve them high to my nephew Raymond.'"

"Oh yes," said Tom. "Uncle Jimmy liked his champagne."

"I really don't approve of that sort of thing." Louise shook her head. "It's living the high life that worried me the most about Jimmy. When he came to visit a few years back, he assured George and I he had practically given up the alcohol. Sure hope he's telling the truth."

Mae was sadly reminded of a very young cousin of hers who had died in a car accident due to a drunk driver. She felt Louise's concern for her brother.

Tom continued. "Well, all I can say — Ray has *ALWAYS* idolized Uncle Jimmy. He used to follow his every move."

"Yes, added Louise, "Jimmy has had a fine musical career."

"I've heard all of the finer hotels in the country have at least two or three of the Philip Morris cigarette girls," said Mae. "He must be doing well for himself. I would certainly love to meet him someday." Mae handed the pictures to Tom.

"You keep the pictures." Tom handed them back. "Give 'em to Ray for me, and he'll probably tell you lots more about Uncle Jimmy."

Mae left the pictures in Ray's bedroom. Later that night Ray was glad the fire escape was secure once again so that he needn't disturb Louise and Mae by entering through the front of the building. The pictures of Uncle Jimmy immediately caught his eye. Before he knew it, Ray found himself contemplating his life so far.

Ray had indeed found a pretty good niche in Maplewood. He had been here 17 years — where had the time gone? Day in and day out, working and building the store and school businesses, connecting with individuals in the community, and playing some music on the side — but he'd once in a while get nagging thoughts. He couldn't rid his mind of the sense that he might have lost something along the way. As he and

Mae seemed to be moving toward a more serious commitment, he needed to carve out a little time alone. He decided to take a weekend trip. He'd travel to Kentucky, and enjoy his memories of Mayfield, Glasgow and Hopkinsville. He would spend some time looking up old friends and classmates, like Leroy and Jack. Quite a few of his friends back home were aware of his success in Maplewood, and would be happy to see him. It was just what he had been needing for quite awhile.

F. A. KENNEDY'S
N E W
5, 10 AND 25 CENT STORE
MAYFIELD, KENTUCKY

| 1915 | | JANUARY | | | 1915 | |
|---|---|---|---|---|---|---|
| SUN. | MON. | TUE. | WED. | THU. | FRI. | SAT. |
| | | | | | 1 | 2 |
| 3 | 4 | 5 | 6 | 7 | 8 | 9 |
| 10 | 11 | 12 | 13 | 14 | 15 | 16 |
| 17 | 18 | 19 | 20 | 21 | 22 | 23 |
| 24 | 25 | 26 | 27 | 28 | 29 | 30 |

~ ~ ~ ~ ~ ~ ~ ~ ~ ~ ~ ~ ~ ~ ~ ~

Summer, 1947

Ray didn't need a map. He drove up to his friend Leroy's house in the tiny town of Glasgow, Kentucky. He knew this area like the back of his hand, and his old grade school friend's house was within walking distance of the house where he grew up. He rang the bell — no one answered. He waited a bit and tried again — still no response. Well, since it was a nice day, he got back in the car and drove to the town square… he rolled down the windows, turned off the engine and breathed in the fresh country air. He had brought along that box of old letters and memories he'd kept stashed away.

Ray's father, Frank Austin Kennedy from Knoxville, a tailor and life insurance salesman, had met Ray's mother, Lula Allen Bittick in St. Louis around the time of the 1904 World's Fair. After Frank married Lula (Louise) in 1905, they lived for a while on Arlington Avenue, and then on Wells Avenue, both in North County. In 1913, however, when Ray was 6 and his brother Tom was just 2, the family left the St. Louis area in favor of the wide open spaces.

Ray found a little calendar from his father and mother — "F. A. Kennedy's New 5, 10, 25c Store, Mayfield, KY. 1914." He also found a business card for "Kennedy's Variety Store, Mayfield KY." The little stores in Mayfield folded by 1917, and Frank was offered another opportunity.

Glasgow became their next home base. Ray was baptized at the Glasgow Baptist Church at age 13. He helped with the family business — another 5 and 10c Store, and this one Frank and Louise managed as a franchise business, under the ownership of H. A. McElroy. They purchased some of their items from Frank's brother, Will Kennedy — or more accurately, from Kennedy Shea Chandler Dry Goods — owned by Will and his partners back in Knoxville. Frank's male customers would choose from a variety of suit fabrics and patterns. Louise's female customers would choose ribbons and hat styles, all from catalogues. The Kennedys would then order the items to be handmade and delivered. H. A. McElroy stocked various and sundry items like reading glasses, Big Chief writing tablets, shower caps, and ladies cosmetics and perfumes. In his free time, Frank played guitar and alto sax with the Glasgow band, which their older son Ray volunteered to reorganize and direct the band while still just in high school. Louise gave piano lessons.

Ray grew up, an aspiring musician who took lessons on both the violin and trumpet. He graduated Glasgow high school in 1927. In those days, a high school diploma was earned upon completion of all course requirements, which often took more than just 4 years, depending upon how much the students were called upon to help their families.

The years came and went, and, although they never starved, Frank had hoped he would do better with sales. So did Mr. McElroy. By 1928 Frank found himself peddling his mail-order tailoring business door to door -- and small town to small town. The dusty roads in Kentucky and Tennessee were taking a toll on his health.

Ray was careful not to tear the old letters as he unfolded them. As he held between his fingers these delicate reminders of the past, he felt for his father. He remembered the quiet, stoic patience Frank had shown — his sheer, hard work. After all, every generation wants something better for their children. Ray decide early in life — if his career ever depended upon him traveling, the work would have to be fun.

Performing with an orchestra on the weekends seemed to fit the definition of great fun. In 1928 he formed the Original Blue Moon Serenaders, from the musicians he'd met along the way, including Leroy and Jack. He also printed up business cards which read, "Ray Kennedy, Private Lessons on the Coronet," and found plenty of students in Glasgow.

He pulled a letter out of the box dated May 26, 1928. Ah — he remembered this adventure quite clearly — his very first weekend orchestra job. He had stepped off the train with his horn, and the Blue Moon Serenaders, in an area known as "Strawberry, KY."

In the Spring of 1928, Ray was a very determined, but also very green, 21 year old. "I sure hope this guy knows what he's doing," Ray thought. "I'm glad to help Mr. Thomas as long as the boys and I get to perform -- somewhere."

Ray was careful with his new music case, recently stenciled with his last name, not allowing it to brush against the strawberry crops. He and the other players trudged across the open field toward their living quarters.

"Hello, Raymond -- it's wonderful to meet you," Mr. Thomas reached out his hand. "We have some nice folks in the nearby towns who'll come hear y'all on weekends. But during your stay this summer, you and the boys here will be expected to assemble the crates, pick the strawberries and keep the neighboring markets well-stocked. Farm labor can be tedious but I have it upon the good word of your father that you and the boys will not slack off."

Ray wrote back home after a few days, about the long drive into the country, sharing a tiny room, with floor mats and no furniture, after full days of making and filling strawberry crates. Oh well -- they'd stick it out through strawberry season. For goodness sake, though -- couldn't stingy Mr. Thomas pay us more than a penny a crate?

By the Fall of 1928, Ray's hopes and dreams were tied to the Blue Moon Serenaders. Many small bands travelled through the South in the late 1920's sharing their music, but many of them were hillbilly bands, unlike the Serenaders. Some of them made it big in radio. As Frank continued to carry his wares from train or bus, door to door, he'd hear from Louise the letters from Ray. His son's trumpet case sounded to Frank like a much lighter, care-free load.

September 26,1928: Ray's letter to his mother, from Crossville, Tennessee on letterhead: *Original Blue Moon Serenaders -- G.R. Holmes Manager; R.H.Kennedy, Director. Music for All Occasions. Glasgow, KY.:*

*Dearest Mom . . .*

*Considering going into the Loop Theatre at Paducah, KY for about 10 weeks. All the salaries will be guaranteed from the start and two nights out of each week will be given to the band, and a few acts of Vaudeville. I think this would be great, don't you? We haven't decided where we will play next week, but I will let you know as soon as I find out for sure. I will also let you know more about the Paducah job later. Will close as I can get this in the next mail. ~ Love, Raymond. P.S. Am sure glad that Dad is getting along so well. I believe the work is good for him.*

Letter from Frank Kennedy to Louise from Columbia, KY, shortly after Ray's letter:

*Darling ~ Have just arrived here, and have found me a very nice room for 50c a night. Think maybe it is the same place that Raymond stopped, but am not sure. I am tired and dusty and have a bad headache. I came over here with a man and his wife, who lives in Louisville and were coming over here. He calls on the banks and seemed awfully nice. They would not accept any pay. It saved me about $1.50 bus fare. The distance to Campbellsville [KY] [from Columbia] is about 20 miles. I intended to come over later in the day on the bus, but was mighty glad to save the bus fare. This is not a very large place and dirty, but hope I will get some business here anyway. I sold an overcoat this morning before I left Campbellsville, and sold two pairs of trousers there yesterday. Think maybe I will sell another suit there Saturday morning if the man gets back from Louisville by then. Hope I will not get typhoid fever. Hope you and Buss [Tom] are okay. Be sure to write me here how you are. Guess I will be here until Friday PM. Is Raymond again at Crossville, Tennessee this week? Honey bunch, you remember the top pattern for the overcoat out of my sample? This is the one I sold this morning. Have not sent in my order yet. Must stay and see what I can do. Be sure to write me. Bushels of love to you and Buss.*

*~ Dad*

The Blue Moon Serenaders were successful with landing that job in Paducah. One evening between song sets, Ray found himself in the company of Plug Kendrick, from WFIW, Hopkinsville, sponsored by Acme Mills.

"It's great meeting you, Mr. Kendrick. I listen to your broadcast every chance I get. I'm a big fan."

"Good to meet you, too, Ray. Just call me Plug. I've really enjoyed hearing you boys this evening."

Plug was a rather wiry, tall, silver-haired man in a grey, pin-striped suit, who moved with an air of graceful, soft-spoken southern confidence. Ray had always admired him as a radio personality. His talent as a broadcaster was undeniable. As the drummer and leader of the WFIW radio band, Plug went out on the road from time to time to find the best talent. WFIW Hopkinsville, one of the earliest radio stations in Kentucky, was holding its own. But Plug could use some help.

After politely shaking hands with the other musicians, Plug pulled Ray aside. "Ray, have you ever thought about working in radio? I don't know how familiar you are with the larger towns, but most have a resident band these days, and we'd like to give you a chance to play and announce on the air."

"Plug, give me your card. I'll talk with the boys and get back with you."

Plug spoke softly. "Ray -- I'm afraid you don't understand. I'm offering *you* a position with WFIW."

~ ~ ~ ~ ~ ~ ~ ~ ~ ~ ~ ~ ~ ~ ~ ~ ~

Ray phoned Louise, back in Glasgow, that same night.

"Hello, Mom."

"Hello, Son -- I hope everything is alright."

"Mom, you'll never believe what happened. You remember the radio program I listen to all the time? You know, the one out of Hopkinsville? They're wanting to give me a chance to work with the radio band, and with the station."

Long pause. "Raymond, your father is not at all well, and I'm very tired."

"Mom -- WFIW is a solid station. And in a town like Hopkinsville there will be more opportunities…"

"Now Raymond, you listen to your mother. By the time I was your age, I had a teaching certificate and a job in an elementary school. It's high time you came back home and helped this family. I've heard about all I care to of the Blue Moon Serenaders. Your father enjoyed playing his alto horn now and again, as you know -- but you don't see him galavanting around playing music now, do you?"

Ray tried to interrupt, "Plug mentioned WFIW is going to become a CBS affiliate. I'll send home a good portion of my paychecks."

Louise spoke over him, "Your father and I have worked very hard, and we're not as young as we used to be. I just don't know how long your father is going to be able to handle this traveling by bus and train from town to town. We're trying our best to make ends meet."

Louise paused to catch her breath. She had an idea. "We're all just going to have to settle down a bit. I don't know why I didn't think about this sooner. Why, with your help we could probably open up a music and hobby shop here in Glasgow. And your brother will appreciate having you around a little more. Now come on back home to Glasgow, son."

Long pause. "I'm not ready to do that just yet."

"Raymond, listen to me!  Your father has always been a bit too soft. I'm putting my foot down. You are *not* moving to Hopkinsville. You *are* coming home."

~ ~ ~ ~ ~ ~ ~ ~ ~ ~ ~ ~ ~ ~ ~ ~ ~

Hopkinsville Newspaper, circa 1929:

*When Plug Kendrick started looking around for an orchestra to make up his Rhythm Millers, he called in Bob Archer, Dewey Shaw, Roger Border, Ray Kennedy,*

*and blues singer, Katherine -- and there you are. If you are at all familiar with the queer and interesting things that happen in the broadcasting world, you will enjoy this story about an orchestra that made good overnight. Some months ago, when WFIW became an associate member of the Columbia Broadcasting system, Director Plug Kendrick felt that his large orchestra was no longer necessary. But all was not well after the musicians were disbanded -- vacant spots appearing. Plug called in Bob Archer, chief announcer, who plays a very totsy fiddle. Announcer Dewey Shaw, who is a hot banjoist, Barn Dance Announcer Roger Border, who toots a clarinet and tenor sax, commercial manager Kennedy, and his blues singer, Katherine, who knows her ivories. The conference resulted in the formation of Plug Kendrick and his Rhythm Millers. With Plug at the drums this band began entertaining daily with popular dance tunes.*

Apr 6, 1930 LETTER from Isabelle Grath, 3422 Hirsch St., Chicago, IL to Ray:

*My Dear Mr. Kennedy ~ Would like to express my sincere appreciation of your entirely fascinating voice over the radio. Please don't take this as the unbalanced raving of a silly chump, tho you would be perfectly justified in doing so. Merely want to let you know that your voice with the soothing lazy Southern accent has given at least one of your long distance hearers great pleasure. Even the long and much repeated talk on insurance sounds like a fairy tale when you tell it. Cannot begin to tell you how much I regret that I shall have so very few more nights in which to listen to your so charming voice and say again how much, how very very much, I appreciate having heard you. Sincerely yours …*

Ray could still feel a twinge of his long-ago excitement, parking his very first car in front of the Acme Mills (home of WFIW), reading the words of this letter over and over, and contemplating what this meant. Ray's radio broadcasting voice was heard and appreciated in places like Chicago! Surely Plug recognized Ray had great potential for the station.

Plug had given Ray several live, on-the-air announcing assignments, along with playing trumpet with the band and singing vocal duets with Katherine the piano player. In those days, Ray would deliver play-by-plays on the air for sporting events (St. Louis Browns, etc). The station hired a reporter to go to the game. He would send what was happening via his telegraph machine, and a teletype machine at the affiliate station (WFIW Hopkinsville in this case) received game information via ticker tape. While Ray waited for the teletype operator in the studio to hand him a transcription based on the ticker tape, it was his job to embellish the story of the game for the radio listeners. Often unbeknownst to the listeners, radio announcers were actually several steps behind the live action of the game. They had to think on their feet and fill in the gaps with interesting banter. As one can imagine, they'd often get it wrong the first time, and would need to fix it somehow. Ray loved it.

He was enjoying himself -- gigs in downtown Hopkinsville, driving to Louisville and other towns with the band on weekends, and, of course -- there was Evelyn.

His mother called him one evening from Glasgow. Ray's father, Frank, had developed a problem with his leg. Louise was seriously contemplating moving her family back to St. Louis. Louise's father was still alive, and a couple of her siblings were living nearby. Instead, Ray offered for Frank, Louise and Tom to come live with him on South Virginia Street in Hopkinsville. They agreed. Louise found a space in the Chickasaw Building where she could give piano lessons. Frank also opened a place — "F. A. Kennedy, Tailoring." And Tom continued his high school studies.

One day, Ray gathered his nerve and decided to share that impressive letter, all the way from Hirsch Street in Chicago, with Plug. Since then, he had received others — one from the Portland, Oregon area. If Ray was building a radio listener following, a raise at WFIW would be in order.

Ray grabbed his things out of the car and went in to work. Plug saw him walk by his office.

"Hey, Taggy -- how many ads did you bring in today?"

"Oh, a couple. Hey, Plug -- when you've got a minute..."

"Not now, Ray. I'm expecting a call. Catch you around lunch time tomorrow."

~ ~ ~ ~ ~ ~ ~ ~ ~ ~ ~ ~ ~ ~ ~ ~

It was a nice walk to Evelyn's house that evening. Spring was in the air, and in his step.

"Hey, baby doll. How are things?"

"Hi, Raymond. You seem mighty chipper."

"Let's take in a movie tonight at the Alhambra. Heck — I'll even buy you a popcorn."

"Let me grab my wrap."

After the movie, they took a little river walk. They talked about the weather. They talked about her beautiful singing voice, and whether she wanted to go with him next weekend to hear Ray, Plug and the other Rhythm Millers in Bowling Green.

The next morning, Plug answered the phone in his usual way. "WFIW Radio -- the very best and bluewing flour station, down in *ooold* Kentucky."

"Hello, Mr. Kendrick, this is CBS Radio. I'm very sorry -- but we need to talk."

Ray arrived a little later. Still no opportunity to talk with Plug. He laid his papers down and noticed a letter on his desk:

*Dear Raymond, Effective Saturday June 14th, your salary will be cut to $20.00 per week, until such time as we are able to acquire more advertising. If this is not satisfactory, I will be pleased to explain the matter to you further.*

Ray was disgusted. Small-town attitudes. Small-town pockets and pocketbooks. Now that the family was yet again trying to lay down roots in a new place, good things just didn't seem to last. Ray loved playing good music, but most of the southern radio stations preferred Hillbilly music, and he was growing tired of the monotony. He thought about his Uncle Jimmy out in Los Angeles and wished he had the means to get there.

Ray and his family owned many phonograph records by now. There was so much hot music to be played. He needed a wider range of opportunity. It was time for a change.

"Mom, I think I'm gonna make a trip back to St. Louis."

"Well son, that's about the best news I've heard in a long time."

In spite of the disappointment with WFIW, Ray would miss Plug. Plug was more than just Ray's boss — he had become a friend and a mentor.

But the WFIW Hopkinsville Rhythm Millers would just need to find a new trumpet player for the radio broadcast.

*Plug wrote Ray several times over the next few years. Ray's addresses on these letters helped trace Ray's whereabouts in the coming years. It's clear from his letters that Plug was fond of Ray, and over the years Ray spoke fondly of Plug and his years at WFIW, Hopkinsville.*

~ ~ ~ ~ ~ ~ ~ ~ ~ ~ ~ ~ ~ ~ ~ ~

Ray, Tom, Louise and Frank were warmly greeted by Grandpa Thomas Bittick, living in North County, who had not seen Louise's boys in quite some time. Ray enjoyed reconnecting with his favorite cousin, "Ollie" (Olney), Uncle Oscar's daughter. He now had frequent opportunities to visit with his Uncles Fred and Oscar. He loved driving to Webster Groves to visit his "Aunt George," (Georgia) and her husband the dentist (Uncle Doc Pitts). Louise's cousins, Sim and Walter, and Walter's wife Margaret, loved to bring their instruments to the family gatherings. Walter played the trombone, Margaret played the saxophone, Grandpa Thomas played the violin, and Louise would play along on Thomas' upright piano.

Ray's apartment on Olive Street was not far from the Lyric Conservatory of St. Louis. The Lyric Conservatory was located on the second floor of the Lorelei Building. The Conservatory offered a weekly radio broadcast *The Stars of Tomorrow*, and Ray was their new Saturday evening program announcer.

Just east of the Lyric Conservatory on Olive Street, Ray's father Frank once again set up a mail-order tailoring business. In the back room, Uncle Fred Bittick ran a bookmaking office, accepting and placing bets on sporting events.

Walter and Margaret, along with their boys, Cliff and Woody, lived in the Tower Grove neighborhood of St. Louis. One day, Walter and Molly took Ray for a drive in Maplewood — a suburb just west of them. By 1931, it had become a destination away from the smog and congestion of the city — a little more green and inviting. It was its own little community, with its own school district, hotel, dance halls, banks, churches and individually-owned businesses — providing most of the conveniences offered in downtown St. Louis and other nearby areas, without the need of a bus or streetcar ride.

In July of 1931, Ray moved into 2246 Blendon Place in Maplewood. His parents and younger brother soon followed him. Ray purchased 50% of the Lyric Conservatory on Olive Street. After renaming it the Mid-west Conservatory, he and his partner sold it three years later, in July of 1934.

Later that same year, in the heart of the Maplewood business district, and in spite of a nation-wide Depression, Ray and Tom Kennedy signed a lease for a large portion of the Maplewood Bank Building, and opened the Kennedy Conservatory of Music.

~ ~ ~ ~ ~ ~ ~ ~ ~ ~ ~ ~ ~ ~ ~ ~

"That's enough reminiscing for now."

Ray closed the box. It was time to get back home. Leroy and Jack, of Glasgow, were no where to be seen this weekend. He felt flushed — not so much from the early-afternoon heat, but from the anticipation. He hoped Mae hadn't gone home this weekend — maybe they could take a little stroll and talk.

Ray was surprised at how excited he was to cross the bridge over the Mississippi River. He admired the impressive St. Louis Riverfront.

Hopkinsville had not led to a broadcasting career in Chicago. And St. Louis wasn't Los Angeles. But maybe, just maybe, Ray could have a good life here — right here in Maplewood.

*Ray lived another 65 years, and throughout those 65 years, he was content to call Maplewood his home.*

# CHAPTER 4
## Dearly Beloved *(Jerome Kern, Johnny Mercer)*

### 1948

"If this is the only way your sister and your mother can see you, then so be it!"   Bertha said sarcastically, as she and Mae walked around the music store.  Hazel joined them, holding her piano music.

"How was your lesson, Hazel?" asked Bertha.

"I don't think I'll *ever* get the hang of it."  Hazel handed her mother her music, and walked over to look through some of the 78 records.

"So your mind is really made up then, Mae?"  Bertha asked, as she turned toward her older daughter.

"It seems like the hours running a business are never-ending; we're dead tired all the time -- but the store and school are both doing well. I'm enjoying ballroom dancing *so* much. Ray's hoping I get good enough to help teach it, like Tom's wife, Mary. And Ray plays his music on the weekends. All in all we're having a great time, Mom."

Bertha was careful to keep part of their conversation private. "And what about those living arrangements -- you sleeping in Ray's mother's apartment..."

"Actually, Ray and Tom are partitioning off a new little section upstairs -- you know, near the big recital hall. There's plenty of room for my chaise lounge, a table or two and a few lamps. I'll show you when we go upstairs -- it'll soon be nice and cozy."

Bertha asked quietly, "You're not getting married in the Church?"

"Yes, we are -- I explained this to you already. It's the Baptist Church practically across the street from the music store."

"You know what I mean, Mae. The nuns have been so good to our family. And Ray is nice enough — I truly enjoy talking with the man — but honestly, he's close to *MY* age! And that mother of his . . ."

"*Shhh* -- Mom, be careful — she's right over there talking on the telephone. Remember I told you she still works here almost every day."

Bertha paused, then leaned in and whispered, "It's just beyond me why a woman so advanced in years ..."

"Is Joe's new girlfriend coming to the wedding?" Mae, feeling more and more awkward, successfully changed the topic.

"I've talked to Joe about that," Bertha replied, "but I just don't know. Jeannie is so shy and quiet -- she barely talks to us. I'm just so glad Joe met Jean. She seems calm — it's good for him to have someone like that. The effects of the war were worse over in Germany than any of us had expected — he will only speak of it with his father — never with me. We're all glad he's back home now. By the way," she reached into her shopping bag, "here's the hat I've bought myself for the ceremony. Do you like it? You'd better wear a head covering -- since I'm assuming from what you say the Baptist Church is still a church..."

"And Louise suggested Buckinghams on Manchester for the wedding brunch. It's on Manchester just a little west of Maplewood. The Kennedys have gone there for special occasions. Fried chicken is their specialty."

"Okay, honey. Your dad and I will call them."

Bertha checked her pocketbook once more for her bus fare. "It's time to go, Hazel. Mae, I think you'll like the dress we made for Hazel to wear on Saturday. Hazel, don't forget we need to measure the hem."

"Okay, Mom."

~ ~ ~ ~ ~ ~ ~ ~ ~ ~ ~ ~ ~ ~ ~ ~

"You're really following through on this? You're marrying that young Catholic girl?"

"Mom...she was raised Catholic. She went with me to meet with the good Reverend at the church you attend about the ceremony. She's really a great gal. C'mon — you already know that. You've spent lots of time with her already."

"Speaking of the ceremony, Ray, please *don't* wear that two-toned tie of yours -- you don't want to look like a playboy casanova at your own wedding."

Tom burst in to the store and broke up the conversation. "An early wedding gift, Ray. You said you always wanted to go but never had the time or the money."

Ray was thrilled when he looked at the tickets. "Tom -- you're a gentleman and a scholar! You shouldn't have -- oh, come to think of it, you really should have!"

"These train tickets are non-refundable so I sure hope Mae still likes you. And we've got people to mind the store while you're gone. So you and Mae don't need to worry about a thing."

Louise walked back over to her desk in the alcove. Ray confided to his brother, "She's the one, Tom. She's such a hard worker, she supports me in everything I want to do — and our kids will be beautiful! She's fine with me playing the trumpet and leading the band down at the Brownsom Hotel on Saturday nights," Ray paused. "Evelyn took it pretty hard, though. I've known her a long time."

"I could tell there really wasn't enough between the two of you. If Evelyn decides to stay here, maybe you could keep her on as a singer with the band — if Mae's okay with it.  All in all, Ray, I like Mae a lot. You've made a good choice."

## August 14

Ray was not normally an early riser, but he found it hard to lie still this morning.  He needed to walk outside for a while, so he decided to drive over to his favorite place.  Chuck, who was now 6, was up and about, so he came along.  They walked along the Mississippi riverbank, skipping stones — Ray deep in thought.  After a few minutes, he reached into his pocket.

"Uncle Ray, where did you get that?"

Ray scratched the bottom of his shoe with the match.

"Oh, this is just an old pipe from my dad's old variety store. I smoke it sometimes. But don't tell your grandma. She always says it's a nasty habit."

"Uncle Ray, what do you remember about Grandpa? I wish I had known him."

Ray paused. As he looked into his nephew's eyes, he wasn't sure what to say about the kind man who had raised him -- the man Ray would have most liked to talk to that morning. The man who had worked tirelessly putting up walls and partitions for the newly-formed Music School. Then, in 1941, without warning, he was gone. Frank Kennedy, while crossing Manchester Avenue in Maplewood, had suffered a massive, fatal heart attack.

Ray was finally ready to answer Chuck's question, and to make that drive back into Maplewood for the big event. "Chuck, I know you never knew your grandpa. He would have loved you. If it weren't for your Grandma and Grandpa Kennedy, why, you probably wouldn't know how to sing, tap dance, or you might not even have that drum outfit to pound on!"

Chuck hesitated, but then asked, "When you and Mae get married -- can I still hang around the store?"

Uncle Ray smiled at his favorite nephew and pulled him close for a hug, "You bet. I need your help there. Say, Chuck — why don't you call her Aunt Mae later today at lunch? She'll like that."

~ ~ ~ ~ ~ ~ ~ ~ ~ ~ ~ ~ ~ ~ ~ ~ ~

As was the custom in those days, the wedding date had been planned to coincide with the bride's mother's birthday. Kennedy Music was closed that Saturday morning. Mae's father walked her down the aisle. No special music -- no big reception. Family and close friends only. They took their vows, and the scriptures and pronouncement were spoken by Reverend Homer Delozier of the Maplewood Baptist Church.

Tom took pictures, and posted them in the Observer newspaper the following week. Louise and her younger sister, Georgia, posed primly and properly. Hazel stood near her mother. Later, at the wedding brunch, Tom toasted the happy couple and gave them a lift to Union Station. Mae in her pink, fitted wedding suit, and Ray proudly donning his two-toned wedding tie, looked like movie stars as they hopped aboard the train, waving goodbye to the camera with twinkling eyes — high hopes of a wonderful life together. The railroad whisked them off toward a Chicago honeymoon.

# CHAPTER 5
## A Couple of Swells *(Irving Berlin)*

The population of the City of Maplewood, around 1950, was 13,000. That might not sound like a lot of people — but consider a typical weekend, when a high percentage of the Maplewood populace either walked, rode the bus, or drove between their favorite retailers along that short portion of Manchester between Sutton and McCausland — not to mention people coming in from the surrounding counties. On a typical shopping day, Maplewoodians could find anything and everything in their hometown. The Maplewood Bank and Trust Company, in the County Observer newspaper, boasted Maplewood had 17 dress shops and 21 shoe stores, along with hat shops, mens furnishings, grocers, butchers, bakeries, drug stores and jewelers — not to mention the doctors, attorneys and optometrists whose offices occupied the second floors. A large number of businesses were unique shops, owned by Maplewood residents. The unspoken loyalty among the merchants, and populace, was to keep "Maplewood dollars" in Maplewood.

The congestion at the Sutton and Manchester Avenue intersection proved difficult when trucks dropped off their wares. Ryan's pub at the southwest corner received frequent deliveries of Budweiser and ice. Since in those days there were fewer stop lights at major intersections, drivers needed to ease around corners yielding the right-of-way to one another. Maplewood was also installing brighter street lamps for late-night shopping, and smoothing the roads with 2-inch-thick asphalt over the out-of-date streetcar rails.

Citizen's Bank bragged about their new drive-up window — the first of its kind west of the Mississippi. The article in the County Observer newspaper appealed to Maplewood housewives by stating the window allowed them to do their banking "in house dress and runnered stockings," from the convenience of their car.

Some of the larger storefronts, such as Goldes, had donned a modern, post-war facelift. And the Maplewood Bank Building facade, still housing Kennedy Music along with Firestone and Dr. Sapian, lost many of its turn-of-the-century curves and filigrees, and took on a more sophisticated, sleek design.

Mae nervously opened the letter from Mr. Fishman, read it silently and then commented. "I can't believe it — *another* rent increase."

Ray peered over her shoulder to take a look. "It doesn't look like too much more this time...and the old building's looking nice. The display windows really look attractive."

Louise was furious. "Ray, it's the principal of the thing. You, Tom and I have been long-time tenants here. He shouldn't be treating us this way."

"Mom, don't take it personally. The man needs to make his money. And we're not the only ones needing to pay higher rent."

"Well, Vera and Johnny Ray and their Beauty Shop have already moved across the street. I think we need to look elsewhere."

The three of them walked over to discuss the situation with Tom next door at the photo studio. "I received the same letter. I've been reading this article about the Claros Corporation, and the new buildings on the 7400 block of Maplewood. It can't hurt to call them and set up an appointment."

The Claros representative met them on a Sunday afternoon at the vacant property at 7417 Manchester. "As you can see, Kennedy Music and the very successful Katz Drug Store would flank both ends of our new Gold Block. And of course, Sears is just across the street."

Ray talked with his brother as they walked around the new property. "We don't want to move too far from the business hub."

The representative overheard. "Mr. Kennedy, it all comes down to word of mouth. Our town is bursting at the seams, and since we're bound in all directions by other townships, our plan is to utilize more of Manchester west of the 7300 block, and more of Sutton Avenue south toward Greenwood. We have great confidence that established businesses, such as yours, will thrive here. And think about this — trying to find a parking space anywhere on Manchester is practically impossible these days. Just *look* at the more-than-ample parking capacity behind these buildings."

"Where would the Music School be? asked Louise.

"Well, available spaces are filling up quickly, but we do own that two-story just around the corner on Marguerette, with an apartment upstairs and an area downstairs easily convertible into individual music studios. All in all, you're getting a great deal on some very attractive property. I'll need to know as soon as possible, Mr. Kennedy."

The property wasn't ideal — not enough square feet remaining for a dance studio — but they needed to do something. Ray and Mae finally had an actual apartment of their own on Marguerette -- a step up from their makeshift living space next to a stage. Tom and Mary still lived on Lohmeyer, and Tom set up a new photo lab inside the music store and remained within easy walking distance of the Observer newspaper on Sutton. Louise insisted she would stay in the 7283a apartment, in the old Maplewood Bank building, unless she could find something more to her liking. And whether Chuck hung out at the store, with his parents or with Grandma Louise, he would have no excuse to be late to his 4th grade class at Lyndover School.

The City of Maplewood hosted a "street party" soon after the Kennedys signed the lease, welcoming the seven businesses comprising Maplewood's new Gold Block. Ray helped provide entertainment for the event.

## 1951

## Come On-A My House *(Ross Bagdasarian, William Saroyan)*

**Sawing Woman in Half Is Easy for Smith; His Tricks Aren't Magic, Just Impossible**

When a stage magician saws a woman in half, pulls a rabbit out of a hat, or makes a table rise from the floor, it's easy to go away mumbling about wires, mirrors, or false bottoms.

But when a man can take a deck of apparently ordinary playing cards and make their spots change, a foot from your nose, explanations don't come so quickly.

**FAVORITES**

Jay B. Smith, Maplewood funeral director, is the latter type of magician. Of course, he can saw a woman in half as well as the next man, but his favorite tricks, and the ones he thinks take the most skill, are tricks done with a standard deck of playing cards. At least, he said it was standard.

*Jay B. Smith*

er patients got sore nurses were always watching magic tricks.

**JACKPOT**

Smith's activities are to formal shows tricks. When Maplewo meters were quite ne ed a group of the some slight-of-hand that made it appear were paying off a six for every nickel he Two days later a citizen appeared at th business and requested refrain from bewilde dren. He said his ready deposited over of Pop's money in pa and was still trying payoff.

**EQUIPMENT**

J. B. Smith, owner and director of the funeral parlor, spent many free moments with the Kennedys just across the street at their new location. J. B. and Chuck shared an interest in Blackstone, the famous magician, so in Chuck's mind, this made all the work of rearranging boxes and boxes of music store inventory worth the trouble. And J. B. already knew Louise and Chuck from Maplewood Baptist Church prior to the move. Mr. Smith was a big help introducing the Kennedys to their new business neighbors. They were now just a few doors east of the Maplewood Public Library, which was in those days located at the northeast corner of Manchester and Big Bend. The large auditorium of the Maplewood Masonic Temple, just west of J. B. Smith's, was familiar to the Kennedys, since it had already been a venue for some of the larger music and dance recitals. If the dance students followed them here, perhaps Ray could work a deal with the Masonic Temple, or possibly the Moose Lodge at Sutton and Elm, for dance rehearsal space.

Louise walked in from around the corner. "Hello, Mr. Smith. Chuck, when you are finished with helping your Aunt Mae, bring me another copy of *Tennessee Waltz* over to the music studio, would you? Your father loves that record so much, and you can teach him to sing it a little later when he gets back. Besides, I haven't seen you since you came home from school today. I miss you!"

"Yes, Ma'am," Chuck said, and quickly put his magic trick cards back in the box as J.B. was getting ready to leave. J.B. walked Louise through the door as he started to make his way back to the funeral parlor.

In a moment everyone could hear a bit of a hubbub happening around the corner. Ray went to open the door, and suddenly Tom appeared, escorting a beautiful woman on his arm.

"Mae," said Tom as he entered the store, "I'd like to introduce you to Rosemary Clooney. She's here for an event this evening for RCA Victor downtown. We thought we'd get a shot or two for the Observer here in the music store."

Mae felt her heart leap. It was her dream, as far back as she could remember, to be a performer. This was not the first time she, Ray and Tom had rubbed shoulders with musical celebrities on their way through the St. Louis area, but it was a genuine thrill for her every time. "It's an honor to meet you, Miss Clooney. We carry all of your recordings."

"Ray and Mae," motioned Tom, "I'll have you stand over here with Miss Clooney -- just in front of the sheet music racks. There — that should be a nice shot."

"Hello, Miss Clooney," Chuck shyly extended his right hand. Chuck so wanted to ask Rosemary Clooney to sing her latest hit, *Come On-a My House*, but just couldn't find the courage to ask her. She leaned down to shake his hand, and smiled.

"Come on, Chuck -- lets get a picture of you and Miss Clooney," Tom said.

"Okay, Pop." Chuck stood as still and tall as he could during the photo. Afterward she turned and gave him a little kiss on the cheek. He blushed.

After the photos, Rosemary Clooney and Tom said their goodbyes. Chuck still felt a little giddy from seeing Rosemary Clooney right there in the music store. Ray reminded him it was time to take the record over to the music school, and spend some time with his Grandma Louise. He walked over to the listening record collection, found a copy of Tennessee Waltz, quickly grabbed his school books and the record, ready to dash out the door — and suddenly the record dropped out of his hands. It fell to the floor and shattered into pieces.

"Chuck, that was a careless thing to do!" Chuck was not used to such a disapproving tone in his uncle's voice. He was a bit frightened.

"Ray it'll be okay," said Mae calmly. "Come on, Chuck — let's pick up the pieces."

The shattered record, in Ray's mind, represented shattered hopes. After a very few months at 7417 Manchester Avenue, it was clear the Gold Block location was not working for Kennedy Music. Ray and Mae were worried. The parking lot was spacious and beautiful, but empty. To pedestrians this strip of stores just west of Sutton Avenue definitely felt like the outskirts of the main shopping area. Kennedy Music was simply not visible to their former Maplewood customers. Ray and Mae would see a few of the music students from their school around the corner purchasing a set of guitar strings or an instruction book, and a few students from Maplewood High School would be drawn in by Mae's clever window displays. For the most part, however, most of the teenagers' pocket change dropped into the Katz Drug Store pinball machines, or onto the lunch counter for a burger and coke. And it was a challenge to stock the store with new merchandise when the income wasn't coming in — so the weekly signs in the display windows gradually changed from smaller, tasteful "store-wide sale" posters to "prices slashed" lettering across giant sheets of butcher paper.

Tensions were also high between Tom and Mary. Mary didn't feel Tom was doing his fair share of raising the children. Tom and Ray talked one day, as Tom stepped out of the dark room.

"Ray, I don't know what to do. Mary has asked me to sign divorce papers. She wants to move back in with her mother down in Texas."

"I'm really sorry to hear that, Tom."

"We've worked out a plan, but it all just seems too quick and too final. Peggy and Mary will move down to Texas with Mary's relatives. I'll keep Chuck with me. Then, during the summer months, we'll want to make sure the kids spend time with each other, and with the other parent. The arrangement is that Chuck goes down there for 6 weeks, and the other 6 weeks Peggy comes up here."

To others, Tom and Mary appeared to have a picture-perfect life. They owned a home together on Lohmeyer Avenue. Tom photographed regularly for the Observer newspaper, and for lots of private events. In the past, Tom and Mary had loved ballroom dancing and participating in regional ballroom events. They had taught dancing, not only at the Kennedy Music, but occasionally in Louise's hometown of Troy, MO. Now that there was no space at Kennedy Music for a dance studio, Mary decided to take a position as an accountant at Schenck Furniture, 7156-58 Manchester, near the Maplewood Theatre.

Tom didn't let on, and certainly didn't want to complain especially to family members, but he was still trying to recover from some disappointments. His prior dream was to travel as a career soldier and take pictures around the world. A slight heart murmur, and his mother's determination to get him discharged, put an end to that dream. Shortly after that, he had a bout with severe anemia which kept him bedridden longer than he expected. And to top all of this off, his very best friend in the world, his cousin Paul Bittick, had recently been killed while serving in the navy. Paul had been a person he could really talk to.

Again, he would never tell another living soul, but he sometimes wondered if his mother was right — maybe she did know better how to live his life than Tom did. Louise tried to always have the final say in both of her boys' lives, and even in her husband's while he was alive.

And now, Louise's opinionated comments regarding Mary were a part of why Mary felt she didn't really belong in Maplewood any more.

"Having Chuck here with me is one bright light in the midst of all of this. I love both kids so much, Ray, and want to be a good father to them, but I just need to figure out what's next. I don't want them to be exposed to this turmoil inside of me."

"I know this is a difficult time for you, Tom. I hate to say it, but Mae and I need to get out of this lease somehow. We've got to find something with a large dance studio, and something we can afford. We'll go broke if we stay here."

The year 1951 could have ended much differently than it did. Ray and Mae could have easily lost Kennedy Music Store and School. Tom could have lost contact with both of his children.

Because of Tom's erratic work hours, Chuck moved in with his Grandma Louise. Louise, now in her early 70's, found Chuck to be a handful at first. Mae's mother, Bertha, told Chuck's grandmother and father that she and John would be happy to have Chuck stay with them a few months during this tough transition time. Chuck attended a school in North County during a portion of the Fall semester of his 4th-grade year. He was soon back in Maplewood, however. He again loved hanging out at Kennedy Music and spending time with his aunt, uncle and grandmother — but missed his dad during those late-evening hours, and certainly hated being so far away from his mother and sister.

As dead-set against divorce as Louise was, she realized down deep she had probably played a part in Tom and Mary's breakup. She sincerely felt guilty. She wanted to make good, and do something to help both of her boys.

---

Louise had an idea. Before leaving for the evening, she picked up the phone at the Music School, and spoke with a very dear cousin.

# CHAPTER 6
## Doggie in the Window *(Bob Merrill)*

### 1953

"Ready, Chuck?"

Mae knew it wouldn't take Chuck much time to grab his jacket. It was a red-letter day for him -- he couldn't wait to hop into the Plymouth with Uncle Ray and Aunt Mae, and see part of downtown St. Louis.

"I'll be ready in a sec!"

By now, Kennedy Music Store and School was well situated at 7179 Manchester — across from the Maplewood Theatre and near the City bus loop — the same loop near the Brownsom Hotel where Mae had stepped off the streetcar eight years previously. Ray's brother, Tom, had just landed a full-time position with MacDonnell Aircraft, and was sent to sunny California on assignment for eight months. Louise had found an apartment at 7167 Lyndover Place, and Chuck had his own room there. Ray and Mae also found a tiny apartment near them at 7210 Lyndover, at Bellevue Avenue. They were all just a stone's throw from the music store and school.

This new music store was much bigger than their previous space on the Gold Block. They could easily resume the dancing school. Their letterhead stationery stated they were "Maplewood's full-service music store" -- musical instruments, records, sheet music, dance and instrumental lessons.

Ray turned to Louise. "Mom, we won't be but a couple of hours. D'ya think you can handle things?"

"I think I should be fine, Raymond," replied Louise. Chuck dashed in from outside, grabbed his jacket and reached down to tie his shoe. "Chuckie, behave yourself in the car this time -- I really mean it."

Chuck lovingly embraced Louise. "Okay, Grandma."

Capitol, MGM, RCA Victor, Columbia and Decca Records each had warehouses in thriving downtown St. Louis. Ray and Mae would drive down to pick up record orders a couple of times a month, and often stopped at St. Louis Music for the latest sheet music.

Chuck had asked his uncle for the keys and dashed on ahead. Mae took the opportunity to walk leisurely with Ray from Kennedy Music to the parking lot.

"Ray, we're going to need a bigger place to live. I read that there are some apartments available on Bellevue."

"What's wrong with our place? I think it's cozy. I guess if Mom and Chuck share a bigger place with us it might not be too expensive . . ."

As they approached the car Mae wanted to be very clear. "Ray, we need our *own* place."

"Let's talk later about that . . . Chuck, you ready to go?"

"You can see I am! Let's go."

Ray knew Chuck loved it when all three of them travelled downtown. He decided to tease him a bit, and winked at Mae. "Mae, are you sure you wanna come along with the two of us?"

"Of course I do, Ray! After all, Chuck and I are a team. I give him the list of new titles, he counts up the 45's and writes up the totals — and I call the record companies to place the orders. All you have to do is pick up the order."

Chuck tried hard to be patient. "That's right, Uncle Ray. Aunt Mae needs to come with us."

"I was just thinking about it again, Grandma might want your help. . ."

Chuck had about all he could take. "Please, Uncle Ray! Grandma already told me she'll be fine. Besides -- while you run in to pick up the boxes, Aunt Mae and I can wait together in the car. You know how hard it is to park around lunch time -- so let's get going."

~ ~ ~ ~ ~ ~ ~ ~ ~ ~ ~ ~ ~ ~ ~ ~

Louise answered the business telephone. "Kennedy Music..."

"Yes, is this the music school?"

"It is."

"And am I speaking with the manager of the music school?"

"Yes, this is Mrs. Kennedy."

"Oh -- pardon my hesitation, but I think I was speaking with someone else by the name of Mrs. Kennedy the other day. . ."

"You mean the sheet music and record clerk. I'm Louise -- the manager of the music school."

"I see -- please forgive me. We're looking for some entertainment just before the annual ballgame of the Fats and Leans, and were wondering, since you've provided this for us before. . ."

"Oh, yes, yes. How are you?" Louise liked adding a dash of bravado to the situation -- her opportunity to shine. "Well, let's see -- of course I'll have to check with the parents, but I think we can assemble a nice group of baton twirlers, along with a talented group of drummers and bugle players -- we call them a Drum and Bugle Corps. I should have more information for you by Friday."

"Yes -- Friday would be perfect. I'll check in with you at the end of the week. Thank you, Mrs. Kennedy, and I do apologize for the confusion."

"You are very welcome. Goodbye, now."

~ ~ ~ ~ ~ ~ ~ ~ ~ ~ ~ ~ ~ ~ ~ ~

"Hey -- Look at the RCA Victor dog, Uncle Ray!"

Mae reached quickly behind her. "Now Chuck, remember what your grandmother said -- sit down in your seat! It's not safe to hang out the window like that while we're driving. They should invent some type of something to keep kids from hanging out of car windows."

Ray agreed. "Stranger things have happened. Listen to your Aunt Mae, Chuck."

Ray pulled up and parked alongside the RCA Victor building. Mae remained in the passenger seat, while Chuck and Ray got out and walked. The 3-foot RCA white smooth-terrier dog was fascinating. He had cute black ears, and a slight, inquisitive tilt to his head. After Ray and Chuck patted "Nipper's" head they proceeded into the large white building (built in the Neoclassical Federal style, like the White House, but on a much smaller scale). They saw another "Nipper" in the lobby -- and this one held his head inside the big brass horn of an old-style gramophone, listening to "His Master's Voice." Chuck was fascinated.

76

"Chuck, run along, now. Get back to the car. Aunt Mae wants to sing with you."

"Okay, Uncle Ray!" Ray watched Chuck as he headed back to the car. He continued to wait as the salesclerk prepared the order.

Chuck had enjoyed coming downtown to the record suppliers since he was tiny enough to stand between Ray and Mae on the wide front seat of the car. "Aunt Mae, I love that old song we used to sing — *The Reluctant Dragon*. Can you help me remember it?"

"Okay, Chuck, let's see if I do —"

Chuck knew, of course, his Aunt Mae would remember every word. She had been singing this song to him as far back as he could remember, with a proper English accent, and by now Chuck always sang along on the choruses. He especially loved the way the melody swooped up at the end on, "whoops, I'm reluctant."

"Okay, Chuck -- since you just took a good look at the big RCA Victor dog, let's sing that song we've been listening to by Patti Page:

'How much is that doggie ...'"

Mae loved bringing a smile to Chuck's face, and her singing voice always did the trick. They always seemed to have a great time together, and Mae admired his wonderful, outgoing personality. She loved how Chuck's exposure to music and performing, through his Uncle Ray and extended family, helped ease the disappointment of being separated from his mother and sister.

A moment or two after they finished the song, Chuck glanced around to see if Uncle Ray was coming. He hesitated to speak but finally asked, "Aunt Mae, do you and Uncle Ray want to move away?"

Mae was shocked and saddened Chuck had overheard her previous comment to Ray, and had mistaken her intent. "Chuck, I hope you know we'd never want to move away from *you*. After all -- you're our *favorite* nephew!"

His face brightened. "Oh, Awwntie Mae," (feigning his best 11-year-old British accent) "I'm your *only* nephew!"

"Well, that's beside the point. By the way, what have you heard from Peggy? How does she like her new school?"

"She *says* she likes it fine -- but I can't wait for her to come up on the train to visit us this summer. She's always talking about the wide-open spaces, all the horses and cattle — maybe I'll learn how to ride a horse on one of my trips down there."

"I'm sure you can't wait to see her. And how's your mother doing? You dad told me Peggy has a new little brother."

"Yes — we call him Skipper. I guess Peggy takes on Paul's last name in school down in Alta Loma. I *think* mother is fine these days — when she and I talk it's mostly about me and school. Peg's stepdad Paul works across the street in a factory. He works long hours, and Peggy says right when the factory whistle blows, she and mother fill the serving plates, call Skipper in to wash up and get ready to sit down for supper when Paul walks through the door — same exact time every evening."

"A little different than around here, isn't it?" Mae knew too well that the music store dinner break hinged around lots of things — the employees' breaks, and whether Ray had a customer or student. "I'm also glad you and she can make those long-distance calls from time to time. You ask your mom to send me another picture of her, okay?"

"Okay."

"Did you hear from your dad this weekend?"

"Yep!  He's really enjoying the weather out in California. Grandma and I have been writing letters to him.  I'm sure hoping he gets back soon, though.  He can't wait to get another dark room set up back here in Maplewood. He's taught me a lot about developing pictures, you know!"

"That's wonderful.  I'm sure glad your grandma helps you with your homework at the music school.  I wouldn't be very helpful with your arithmetic, but maybe with your story writing."

"And guess what Grandma Louise did?  She wanted me to have a nice place for my books, so she asked the nice man at the Maplewood woodworking shop to build a bookcase for me!  I wrote Peggy about it and she couldn't believe it.  She says I'm spoiled."

"Are you talking about the man who has a shop by the Footlong Hotdog, near Manchester and Bellevue?  He always sits near the window of his shop while he carves — I guess so everyone can see him."

"That's the place.  He even gave me a little carved dog made from the scraps. He's a really nice man."

"Chuck, I'm sure you and your Uncle Ray will be spending lots of time together very soon.  He doesn't know it yet — let's keep this our little secret — but I'm going to need to take a little break from the music store, and Uncle Ray will really need your help.  Do you think you can do that for us?"

"Aunt Mae, you can count on me."

They could see Ray was making his way back to the car.  Mae asked Chuck to open the back door as Ray laid the heavy record boxes into the car next to Chuck.  "Chuck, time for White Castles!"

"Hooray!"

~ ~ ~ ~ ~ ~ ~ ~ ~ ~ ~ ~ ~ ~ ~ ~ ~

The White Castle on Vandeventer Avenue, near where Chouteau and Manchester Avenues intersect, was their favorite spot to stop on the way back to the music store. Normally they would all go in and eat — but Mae didn't feel like eating just yet. On the back seat Chuck juggled orange sodas and a bag of burgers — keeping the orange soda away from the records was enough to keep him sitting relatively still.

"Uncle Ray, we didn't see the giant birthday cake this time on the way back."

"That's because we didn't take the Express Highway. Mae sometimes likes it better when we take Manchester Avenue all the way in."

"What do you mean about the birthday cake, Chuck?" Mae asked.

Ray explained, "There's a big Standard Station there at McCausland Avenue and the highway. Do you remember how we turn south there? Chuck used to think, when he was tiny, that Standard had painted a giant birthday cake on the sign, just for him. It has a giant candle on it — remember, Mae?"

"Oh, I *do* remember that, Ray! They painted it there just for my special nephew."

"Aunt Mae, you probably won't like what Mr. Collins said at school yesterday. He said they might extend the Express Highway. That way people can get to places like Brentwood and Rock Hill, without having to stop at every light along the way." Aunt Mae, maybe Uncle Ray should teach both you and me how to drive!"

"You're right, Chuck. I am in no rush for faster-moving cars." Mae was still more comfortable with public transportation, and often took the bus when Ray wasn't available to drive her places.

"Aunt Mae, maybe Uncle Ray should teach both you and me how to drive!"

Manchester Avenue brought them directly into Maplewood, and Ray found a space in front of the store to unload the records.

"Ray, I don't think I'll have any food right now. I'll help your mom while you and Chuck take a lunch break."

Mae felt a little twinge in her side as she turned to reach for a box of records. "Maybe Chuck can help bring in some of these."

Concerned, Ray told her to wait, shut off the engine and helped Mae into the store first, before he and Chuck unloaded the record boxes.

"You okay? You look a little pale," Ray asked.

"Just car sick, I guess."

"You probably need to eat."

"Yes — but just give me a couple of minutes."

Louise approached Mae as she walked in.

"Did you speak with the Fats and Leans Committee last week?"

Mae walked slowly with Louise back toward her desk. "Yes, Louise -- I meant to tell you all about it. They stopped in regarding entertainment for the annual ballgame."

"Well," Louise's tone seemed even more imperious than usual, "when anyone calls about such things pertaining to the music school, they need to speak with *me*."

"Of course," Mae quickly retorted. "I wouldn't have it any other way." Mae was in no mood for a confrontation.

Louise wouldn't drop it. "I just don't know how the man got the idea that *you* were the manager of the music school."

"I can assure you, Louise -- I certainly had no intention of making him think that."

"You know, I am perfectly capable of managing these things. You wouldn't know the first thing about how I've done it in the past . . ."

"I just gave the man our phone number. . ."

"Let me finish, please." Louise was insistent. "I realize, Mae, that you are new to this family, and to the business. Believe me, after you have done this as many years as we have, you will realize that organizations in the community, like the Fats and Leans, depend upon the local businesses to do their part in assisting the underprivileged in our area."

Mae was beginning to see spots as she made her way to the stool near Louise's desk so she could take a seat. "I'm sorry, Louise. Next year, I'll just ask the man to come by and see you personally."

Louise paused -- she couldn't argue with that kind of reasoning. The tone of her voice relaxed a bit. "Yes -- the personal contact with the community. That's something Ray, Tom and I are good at. By the way, you really should work to improve your dancing skills -- if you could just learn to teach dance, the way Mary did. . ."

"I'm enjoying getting to know Cliff and Woody Brown. Have you seen them around today?" Mae interjected. There were many times over the years that Mae had learned to redirect Louise's conversations in order to keep the peace.

"Mae, it was truly a miracle the way things worked out for the Browns and for the Kennedys."

"Cliff and Woody are Tom and Ray's cousins, correct?" Mae knew this, of course. Anything to keep the conversation light.

"Technically, their father, Sim Brown, and his brother, Walter, are cousins of mine. Walter is a dear fellow — if you recall, he was the streetcar conductor who used to ring the bell for me when he stopped at Oakview Terrace in front of our old location. It's Sim's two boys I'm talking about — very good boys. I doubt if you've heard the entire story, and so I'll tell it to you now. A few months back, while we were struggling to keep our heads above water, I overheard Ray and Tom talking, and I had a thought. I phoned Walter. I told him we were in a very tight bind. Walter told me Cliff and Woody's store, Brownie Music Store over on Ivanhoe, although very attractive, just wasn't drawing in the business they had hoped it would. Walter had a talk with Sim, and soon after that, Woody and Cliff spoke with Ray about pooling our resources. In turn for them helping us end the old lease, and rent this wonderful building, we invited them to merge their business with ours. I don't know what we would have done without their help."

"That was a brilliant idea of yours, Louise."

"Divine inspiration is more like it. You and Ray should come join me for church more often. I don't know that Cliff and Woody will work here on a daily basis — they're young and relatively new to owning a music store — but we'll see. " Louise's expression began to change — Mae could tell the conversation would not remain pleasant.

"Family is so important, Mae — why, I just don't know where Ray and Tom would be today if it hadn't been for my influence. I waited to tell you this, but you and I should be honest with one another. Just so you know -- Ray would never have married and settled down with you if it hadn't been for me. Tom's wife, Mary, just wasn't right for him from the beginning, but I could see a wonderful change in Ray from the moment he met you. You might as well know — the only reason Ray married you, and settled down, was because I wanted him to. He would have continued to play the field, but he needed that stability in his life. I told him so. You have me to thank for it."

Mae was silent — speechless. What a thing to say -- it wasn't Ray's own idea to marry her? And Mary was one of the nicest people Mae had ever met — how could Louise think she wasn't right for Tom? It had been apparent from the beginning of Mae's marriage that whatever Louise said was never disputed by either of her sons. She certainly had them both wrapped around her little finger. But what Louise just said couldn't have an ounce of truth in it ... could it? Before she had time to think of how to reply, Ray and Chuck made their way back to Louise's desk. "Here are your White Castles, Aunt Mae! They're getting cold."

Her nose was invaded by a horrid smell of the White Castle burgers wafting up and intermingling with odors of all types (guitars, records, music books, her own sweat). Suddenly she felt the room spin. She backed away from the food in Chuck's hand, and hoped she could get herself to the bathroom on time.

~ ~ ~ ~ ~ ~ ~ ~ ~ ~ ~ ~ ~ ~ ~ ~

That evening she was feeling much better. Even a bit hungry. She snuggled next to Ray, watching Sid Caesar on their brand new television. The popcorn tasted good.

Mae wanted so badly to speak frankly with Ray about what Louise had said, but she knew how close he was to her. Conversations about Ray and his mother never seemed to go anywhere.

In Mae's peripheral vision, she thought she saw something that didn't look like popcorn in Ray's hand. She turned her head toward him. "What was that?"

"What was what," Ray asked, still staring at the screen. His hand was back in the popcorn.

She grabbed another piece of popcorn. "Oh, nothing...I guess."

Mae and Ray laughed at Imogene Coca. It was good to relax at the end of the day. Her legs started to cramp because of the long hours on her feet.

"Ray, would you rub my toes — now wait a minute — what was that?

"What was what?" Ray asked. Mae noticed a slight smirk on Ray's lips.

"Okay, what's going on?"

"I really don't know what you mean. Here — let me see your lower leg, and I'll get your toes while I'm at it." His eyes twinkled.

"You would tell me if you were eating something else — wouldn't you, Ray?"

"Well of course I would, Geranium!"

She reached around him, and after finding just the right tickle spot, he revealed the half-eaten box of Oreos.

"I was saving half of them for you, honey bunch!"

"It's a good thing. I've been waiting for the perfect time to tell you. I saw Dr. Ott yesterday and it's official — I'm eating for two now."

# CHAPTER 7
## Mr. Sandman *(Pat Ballard)*

### 1954

It is hard to fathom now how we ever did without it, but air conditioning is a relatively new invention. In the mid 1950's, finding an air-conditioned space was still rather a hit-and-miss thing. There were a few places where you could count on it — movie theaters were a sure bet. During the 50's, for the price of one movie ticket, you got a double feature (two full-length movies), with cartoons and newsreels in between — and a comfy, cool place to be entertained, or to catch up on missed sleep, on a summer afternoon.

During mid-July, 1954, stepping outside after the double feature was unusually difficult. For several days straight, soles of people's shoes seemed to stick to the tar pavement. You could fry an egg on the top of your car. There were several evenings when temperatures were still in the 90's at bedtime, and families would sleep outside in their backyards, or drive to Art Hill in Forest Park and sleep there. The St. Louis Post-Dispatch weather bird had a weary, limp expression on his face for several days straight.

The summer of 1954, still to this day, holds the record as the hottest summer ever in the City of St. Louis.

Ray and Dr. Ott and Bill Harper (owner of Harpers Photography) tried to find a shady spot, and a bit of a breeze, outside the Cape-Harper Building at Sutton and Maple. They were comparing the latest cigars Mr. Harper had set aside.

"I told Mae it could be any day now," said Dr. Ott. "Does she have her suitcase packed, Ray?"

Ray nodded as he took a long draw on his stogie. He had unbuttoned his top few shirt buttons in order to loosely wrap a white handkerchief around his neck. "Mae looks like she's about to pop. And this heat is unbearable for her. Can't you move things along for her, Doc?"

"Is it St. Mary's Hospital you're planning on? Just be sure and have the hospital call me when she gets there."

"Better top off the ethyl in the car tonight, Ray," said Bill Harper.

On the morning of Monday, July 12, just across from the Maplewood Theatre, Kennedy Music was far from cool and comfortable — the tall fans noisily wafted up the warm air and swirled it around. Ladies held on to their skirts and loose-fitting blouses as they made their way in and out of the front door. Mae, in her flattest shoes, couldn't care less if the hem of her maternity dress flapped about. She walked wearily around the sheet music racks, attempting to finish placing the newly-lettered cardboard dividers into the slots, and couldn't wait for something more to drink.

Ray had just returned from Harpers Photography.

Mae fanned herself with a piece of sheet music as she spoke. "Ray, I might need to leave early today. I really can't take it."

"And *I* really think I should take you home," Ray said nervously. "Sit down, now, and drink more cold water. Let's prop your feet up. I want you to be careful."

Around noon, Ray helped his very pregnant wife into the car, and they drove to the Steak and Shake in Rock Hill. She ordered a Coke over ice — the coldest thing she could think of.

Shortly after, Mae knew it was time. Ray helped her back into the car, and they made their way back to St. Mary's Hospital in Clayton. On Mae's behalf, the hospital put in a call to Dr. Ott.

The nurses assured Ray he could go back to work — they assured him that first babies normally took some time. He gave Mae a kiss before leaving. "I'll be sure to call your parents, and let Bertha and John know how things are going this evening. Don't you worry."

"Don't you worry either, Ray. Get back to work, now."

The labor room was extremely hot, despite the presence of electric fans. Labor at the hospital was not private — several mothers-to-be shared a room. Being confined to plastic-covered mattresses and sweaty bedsheets was no picnic in the park. Every woman in the labor room that day hoped and prayed the sun would go down a little earlier. They were comforted by nurses and aides in starched uniforms. In spite of all the discomfort, Mae felt more secure to be here under a nurse's care, than to give birth at home, as her mother and grandmother did.

"Here honey," Mae opened her eyes — the nurse had just finished soothing her eyes and forehead with a wet cloth. "I'm putting a little ether on this cotton ball, and I'm strapping it to your wrist. When you just can't bear the pain, bring this cotton to your nose, and it'll help you."

"Okay." Mae groaned, weakly. She tried the ether, and it just made the room spin around her. She couldn't decide which was the worst part — the thirst, the closeness of the room, the wet sheets, the distressed calls of women in beds close by, her intensifying pain and nausea.

The family gathered in the waiting room. Louise needed to be home with Chuck, but Bertha and John shared cigarettes and coffee with Ray into the night.

"How's my wife Mae?" Ray nervously asked the nurse passing by.

"Hello, Mr. Kennedy. Your lovely wife is doing just fine. We still can't seem to reach Dr. Ott, though. But don't be concerned — she's in good hands here."

"Where *IS* that dad-blamed Dr. Ott?" Ray exclaimed. He nervously fumbled for another cigarette.

The twilight sleep method of childbirth was in vogue in 1954. A first-time mother had many long hours of hard labor. Then, at the moment of birth, after she was rolled into the delivery room, a gas mask was applied. The twilight effect of a painless delivery, also meant the mother wouldn't remember the moment of the baby's first cry — but it was the best relief available.

Around 1:00 am, the nurse said, "Honey, it's time. You are fully dilated. The nurse looked around — still no sign of Dr. Ott. As the gurney rolled down the hall, Mae was worried. What will happen if the doctor doesn't arrive on time. . .

"Goodnight, Mae." Suddenly she was under.

On July 13, at 2:00 am, Ray and Mae became proud parents of a baby girl.

~ ~ ~ ~ ~ ~ ~ ~ ~ ~ ~ ~ ~ ~ ~ ~ ~

Tom wrote to his brother. He congratulated Ray for becoming a first-time father at the age of 46. He couldn't wait to see pictures of little Wanda. Then Tom wrote a little note to his mother and Chuck, telling them to come out soon for a visit in sunny Los Angeles, California. Disneyland was being built — and in the meantime Knotts Berry Farm looked to be a fun place for Chuck to explore. And although it would be hard for Ray to get away with a new baby, this would be an opportunity for Chuck to meet his Uncle Jimmy, before school started. Uncle Jimmy was Louise's famous brother who had played the drums and led orchestras on the West Coast in his younger days. Tom promised Chuck and Louise he'd take them to all of the fun places Uncle Jimmy had told him about, like the Coconut Grove and the Brown Derby. Staying in California while working for MacDonnell Aircraft made Tom feel homesick, especially over those long weekends.

~ ~ ~ ~ ~ ~ ~ ~ ~ ~ ~ ~ ~ ~ ~ ~ ~

Bertha and John came to visit Mae. They brought along a beautiful bassinet for baby Wanda Rae.

"Just look at the poor little thing," exclaimed Bertha. She's completely covered with heat rash. This summer is unbearable."

Mae freshened and re-hung the damp towel near the window fan. John was in his t-shirt as Bertha took a picture of baby and grandpa.

"Thanks for bringing it by, Mom."

"I'm just glad Hazel's baby Robbie Sue is old enough she doesn't need it anymore." said Bertha.

# CHAPTER 8
## Adorable *(The Drifters)*

Thanksgiving, 1955

A bleary-eyed Peggy got out of bed, walked over to the desk in the living room and grabbed a pencil and some paper. Chuck noticed when she walked into what had become his bedroom, and told her to switch out the pencil, since he needed the better eraser for school next week. She began to write:

*Dear Mommy,*

*You know Grandma [Louise] says if we want to sleep in the morning that we are off of school, we have to sleep until <u>she</u> gets up. And I sleep next to her (woe is me). Every move I make she looks at me — and I wanted to use the bathroom and* *she said 'no.' But a little later she let me use it. Well, Grandma just let us get up and it is about 12:00 o'clock. I am writing a longer letter than I ever did. But I can think of more to say, I guess.*

*Chuck got his package and he likes it very much. But we are moving to 2510 Bellevue next week. I will write and tell you as soon as we move. Hey, you better write more often, even if I don't. After all I have to go to school (ha ha ha).*

*Down there [in Texas] we eat a lot, but up here the restaurant food doesn't taste so good, so I don't eat too much and, besides, the [cold] air just takes away my appetite.*

*Down at Goldes there's a little Santa Claus in the window and it is real cute. It talks to you. It asks your name and then he repeats it. He says he will bring you a present, whatever you want for Christmas.*

*I sure wish I was there — you said you are about to 'go mad' without me. Well, I am even about to 'go madder' without you, although I am enjoying it up here. But as you always said, Texas is better.*

*We go skating every Saturday, though. Daddy is going to buy me a skating outfit.*

*I cannot wait til Christmas can you? I'm so glad you got your trunk. I sent Skippy a <u>late</u> birthday card — did you get it?*

*Chuck and I are saving Eagle Stamps so if you do not have a book, please get them and send them to us. We can't save $3.00 for a magic set because we've got to save our money for the Christmas presents down there. We always see something we want, and so Chuck just has to get it, and me too sometimes. And when he sees something he wants and don't have the money, I always lend it to him. And every Friday there is a good show on, and we have to pay our way in. So you see it is hard for us to save our money.*

*Dear Mommy I heard over at the music store the record called 'The Littlest Angel' and it was real pretty. I am getting two more records — 'Just a Closer Walk with Thee' and 'There will be Peace in the Valley.' They are both by Red Foley. And if you hear 'Cattle Call' tell me if I should get it. If there are any others you would like just let me know cause I can get them at half price.*

*Well, tell everybody hello and I miss everybody. Tell everybody if they will write to me I will write to them.*

*Well, my hand is getting sore from holding a pencil, so goodbye, long letter.*

*Love and kisses,*
*Sissy.*

Whew — a lot of writing and erasing! Peggy's whole body felt cramped.

"Nice penmanship. Very nice." Louise was finally up and about. "Peggy, honey, you'd better get dressed. And remember, wear something nice for Aunt George."

Peggy dug around in the little closet which she shared with Chuck. She bumped into Chuck a few times while he tried to fix his tie.

Sixth grade was turning out to be okay. Even though Peggy didn't know many of the kids yet, she did enjoy walking to Lyndover School with Chuck and hanging out at the music store in the afternoons. But today was certainly different — a Thanksgiving away from her momma.

Tom honked the horn outside for them. Louise enjoyed the car ride and conversation, as Chuck, Peggy and Tom talked all the way to Webster Groves, along Manchester and Big Bend Avenues.

Aunt George owned Georgette's Beauty Shop at the corner of Big Bend and Berry Road in Webster Groves, as far back as Chuck and Peggy could remember.

Louise straightened Chuck's tie and then rang the doorbell. "Hi, Sis — come right on in, everyone. Ray, Mae and Wanda have already arrived. They're in the living room."

By 1955, Georgia had been widowed a long time. It was wonderful she and Doc Pitts had purchased this home so many years ago, which allowed her the luxury of working from home and forming many long-time friendships with her beauty clients. Unlike Louise, Georgia never had children, and it was a delight for her to entertain her two nephews and their families.

Chuck and Peggy asked their Aunt George if they could walk through the beauty shop. The part of the shop they liked best was at the front of the house. The front wall was all windows, so the room was often very bright. There were four vanities with large mirrors, which Georgia had collected throughout her many years of working as a beautician. Standing up in the corner was a yard stick with a little magnet at the bottom, held together by a twisted metal cord. Peggy picked up the yard stick.

"I'll pick up the bobbie pins, Aunt George."

"No need to do that today, Peggy. I think I got 'em all yesterday. Thank you, though!"

"Yep — here's one!" Peggy was excited to have found a small but ornate hat pin lying just next to a vanity leg.

"You have very good eyes, Peggy! Thank you. Mrs. Kleineschmidt will be very happy to get that nice pin back." Peggy noticed, as she handed the pin to her, that Aunt George's right-hand thumb and index finger nails were peculiarly arched and worn looking. Over the years Aunt George had perfected a technique of using her front teeth, along with these two fingers, to open and maneuver the pins as she worked.

They walked into what Aunt George called the washing and drying room next — a bigger room with several bouffant hair dryers attached to the backs of overstuffed, deep green colored chairs. The basins Georgia used for hair washing were along the south wall.

After the beauty shop tour, everyone squeezed in around the small dining table. It was time for photos of the feast and of the family. Shots were alternately taken by Tom, Ray and Chuck. After pumpkin pie, Aunt George moved everyone into the living room and decided it was her turn to hold baby Wanda.

"Peg, let's go outside and play in the leaves — Grandma, may we be excused?"

"Sure, Chuck — stay in the yard, though.  Don't wander off."

Peggy couldn't wait for Christmas.  She yearned to visit her mother and her half-brother, Skipper, who had been born in Texas — and to open presents under the tree with both brothers.  Everything would be so much better if everyone lived in the same place, and she fully thought that this year it was going to happen.  After all, Momma had told her so.

"Peg, let's both call mother and Skip tonight and ask about their Thanksgiving."

"You knew just what I was thinking about, Chuck!"

~ ~ ~ ~ ~ ~ ~ ~ ~ ~ ~ ~ ~ ~ ~ ~

In just a few short weeks, Peggy hugged Marion Knapp, her best friend at Lyndover School.  She assured her she'd be back after the Christmas break.

Peggy and Chuck packed their bags — they had carefully wrapped the little gifts for their momma, little brother and stepdad, and stuffed them in.

It was always a great adventure driving with their daddy to Union Station.  He would walk them down the long tunnel to the train headed for Houston.  There were never enough long hugs and goodbyes, and by the time they found their seats this time, the conductor was already checking tickets.

Chuck and Peggy felt free, sitting on the train side by side, with no one to interrupt their long conversations.

"I just don't understand it — mother and Skip seemed to enjoy being in Maplewood at the beginning of the school year.  I thought she liked her new job."

Peggy was thoughtful in her response. "Well, the job was fine, and the apartment looked just fine to me. I think she was just homesick."

"I'll bet it's just colder here than she likes it. At least that's what Daddy said."

"That's probably it." Peggy was remembering her high hopes that summer. As usual, Chuck had travelled down to Alta Loma, Texas for his six-week visit with Peggy and Mary. And when his visit was over, Mary travelled back to Maplewood with Chuck, Peggy, Skipper and a trunk of belongings. She surprised Ray and Mae with a visit to the music store. Tom was overjoyed Mary was back in town. And then, in just a few short weeks, she returned back down to Alta Loma with Skipper.

Prior to her return, Mary tearfully asked Peggy if she wanted to remain at Lyndover School in Maplewood for the semester, or if she wanted to come home with her. Peggy was confused and hurt by her mother's change of heart. Why did "home" need to be a place so far away from her brother Chuck, and from her daddy? She was angry, and told her momma in no uncertain terms that she *did* want to finish, not only the semester but also the entire school year, in Maplewood with her daddy and big brother. But by the time Thanksgiving rolled around, she missed her momma something fierce. Maybe, just maybe, if Peggy could just learn to control her temper, her momma and little brother would move back to Maplewood for good. And telling Chuck about all of this would upset him -- and maybe make things worse.

The view from the train, St. Louis to Houston, was beautiful during the holidays, especially at night. As the two kids travelled farther and farther south, there was no sign of snow — but every tiny town along the route was decked in beautiful Christmas decorations, from the first street light to the last, along each Main Street. They were overjoyed to see their mother at the depot, and after many hugs they climbed into the back of the car and road the 50 miles back to Alta Loma.

Even though Chuck missed a snowy Christmas back home, he enjoyed his visit with Skipper. Mary loved the records Peggy had chosen for her from the music store. Not one of them had broken in her little suitcase. Peggy helped her momma serve up the ham and mashed potatoes. After dinner, Chuck entertained the family — he played his ukelele and sang some Christmas carols while everyone joined in. When the time came to finally open his gift of a new magic set, he dazzled his little step brother with some card tricks, using the new deck inside the box.

The time to travel back to St. Louis after Christmas came all too soon. The night before, both kids packed up their cases and went to bed early — Chuck in a room with his younger brother, and Peggy in her own room.

Peggy heard a familiar knock on the door, and a quiet turn of the door knob. She was quite groggy, but opened her eyes when she realized who it was.

Paul sat down on the side of the bed. "Well now — your momma says you've been liking that school in St. Louis."

Peggy yawned. "It's okay, I guess."

Mary called softly across the hallway. "Peggy, you in bed? Everything okay?"

Paul answered her quickly. "She's fine, Mary. I'm just tucking her in." He moved closer. Peggy pulled herself up in bed, trying to wake up.

"You know, Margaret, your mother was very upset when you decided to stay in St. Louis the last few weeks. Very upset. I've never seen her cry more than when you refused to come back home with your mother."

Peggy was certainly wide awake now. She didn't want to say too much. Did he know about the tantrum she'd thrown when her momma decided to move back to Texas just a few weeks ago? Paul did not tolerate tantrums. She felt butterflies in her stomach.

"And I really don't like your mother being that upset. So I've decided something."

Peggy had a sinking feeling inside — when Paul spoke in that way, she knew there was a punishment coming.

"I've decided, Margaret, that if you decide to live up there again — leave your mother — even for just a little while — you'll never see your mother again."

A wave of pain and fear shot through her.

Paul continued. "Chuck just needs to run along back home tomorrow, and you can keep quiet about our little conversation. You'll just stay here with your brother Skipper tomorrow. Your mother needs your help looking after him anyway, while she drives Chuck to the train station. You can place a call to your father in the morning, after you've told your mother you've made a change of plans. Is that clear?"

"Yes, sir."

He left the room.

~ ~ ~ ~ ~ ~ ~ ~ ~ ~ ~ ~ ~ ~ ~ ~

Circa 1930: Early in his career, Ray announced and performed on WFIW Radio, located at the site of Acme Mills, Hopkinsville, Kentucky.

Plug Kendrick offered Ray a position at the station, and they remained close friends after Ray moved to Maplewood.

The Mid-West Conservatory, also called the Lyric Conservatory, was located on the second floor of the Lorelei Building in the St. Louis (still stands today). Ray began working there just after moving to St. Louis from Hopkinsville, and soon co-owned the Conservatory. The Lorelei building also had a huge ballroom on the bottom floor, which opened over an Olympic-size swimming pool.

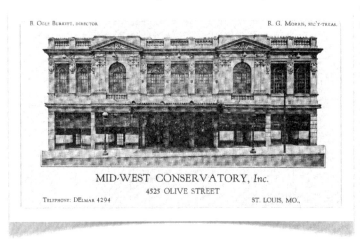

B. OGLE BURKITT, DIRECTOR                    R. G. MORRIS, SEC'Y-TREAS.

MID-WEST CONSERVATORY, Inc.
4525 OLIVE STREET
TELEPHONE: DELMAR 4294                    ST. LOUIS, MO.,

Circa 1933:
Frank Kennedy's Tailor Shop on Olive Street, just down the street from the Midwest Conservatory. Ray and Frank travelled together by streetcar to and from work. Fred Bittick, his brother-in-law, was a bookmaker in Frank's back office.

Frank helped construct partitions for Kennedy Music at their first location in the Maplewood Bank Building.

Tom Kennedy, circa 1934, in front of the first location of Kennedy Conservatory in Maplewood. Ray taught various musical instruments; Tom taught dancing.

1939:
First picture taken inside Kennedy Music and Hobby Shop, 7281 Manchester Avenue. Left to right: Frank, Louise, Tom and Mary Kennedy. Tom also owned a photography shop next door.

1939: Ray and a customer inside the first Kennedy Music location.

Ray loved to perform in the St. Louis area prior to owning a store in Maplewood. During the 1930's he led orchestras at the Brownsom Hotel ballroom at the City Limits Loop, and at a dance hall located in 7314 Manchester (now Vom Fass). He played at an establishment owned by Ben Gross, and at Concordia Turner Hall on Arsenal Street, as well as the Highlands amusement park near Forest Park.

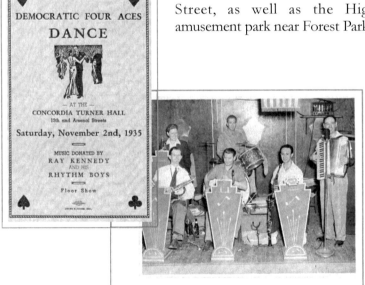

Circa 1934. Louise Kennedy directed dramatics, both at Kennedy School of Music, and at the Maplewood Baptist Church. Ray and Louise (back row) and Tom (seated center) were among the players in this production.

In August, 1934, Ray and Tom also participated in St. Louis Municipal Opera's production of "My Maryland." They walked on stage as part of a Muni-sized orchestra comprised of local musicians.

1938:
Edith Mae Heimberger, age 11, with Grandma Kitchen and Uncle Louie, Bertha's mother and brother. Ironton, MO.

Circa 1945: Edith Mae Heimberger, when she and Ray were first getting acquainted.

1948:
Ray and Mae in their first makeshift apartment, near a stage in the upper floor of the original Maplewood Bank building.

1940's: Chase Park Plaza. Tom and Mary, along with Mae and Ray. Seated with them is Fred Lowery, famous blind whistler recording artist, and his companion.

Ray and a group of students standing in front of F. W. Woolworth's, 7366-7368 Manchester Avenue. advertising the Fats and Leans Carnival.

The Fats and Leans were a Maplewood charitable organization, sponsoring a baseball game and carnival every year to raise funds to help children and youth in need.

Photo left:
Annual Fats and Leans ballgame, Sutton and Lyndover, now Ryan Hummert Memorial Park.

Circa 1951: Maplewood Christmas Parade.

*Kennedy-Brownie* became the name of the music store when related cousins temporarily formed a partnership.

Local television broadcast. By the looks of the backdrop, Mae's interview was most likely on behalf of Kennedy Music.

1950's photo of the Maple-wood Theatre. Note the marquee: children were free when accompanied by parent. One ticket usually purchased two full-length movies. Ray Kennedy always called the Maplewood Theatre *the picture show.*

Circa 1960, Chuck holds a camera from which double slides were developed, for use in a special 3-D stereoscope viewer. Chuck and his dad, Tom Kennedy, were wedding and special event photographers around the St. Louis area.

Circa 1962: Ray, Mae and Ray Jr. at 7394 Maple Avenue, the second house east of Sutton, across from Harpers Photo. This house, and the house just east of it, were torn down and replaced by an apartment complex in later years.

# Kennedy Music School Recital Venues

Maplewood Richmond-Heights High School

7291 Manchester, Maplewood Bank Building 2nd floor

# Lyndover School

Louise and an instructor, 2643 Marguerette, around 1950. Because the music studios were too small to hold dance classes, dance instruction was either on hold temporarily, or was held at the Masonic Temple across Manchester. The 2nd floor was Ray and Mae's first real apartment.

Maplewood Masonic Temple
7468 Manchester Avenue at Big Bend

Moose Lodge
Sutton Blvd. at Elm

The Admiral
St. Louis Riverfront

Chuck, far right, is the Pied Piper. Wanda, 2nd row closest to camera, is part of the childrens' chorus.

## 2707 Marshall Avenue
### between Manchester and Marietta

Circa 1975: Inside photo of Kennedy Music, 7310 Manchester

Same year: Bob Heimberger, in an outside view of same building during a sidewalk upgrade. Note the Kmart parking lot across the street.

7320 Vine Street
Built in 1904, home of the Ray and Mae Kennedy 1966 through 1996.

Inside the house on Vine St. Mae had just constructed a bookcase to cover a doorway. The upright bass in front of the bookcase belonged to their youngest son, Tom. This room served more as a music room than a dining room.

## Above:

Photo of Harper's, taken during the 1970's. Dr. Ott, our family practitioner, had an office on the 2nd floor.

## Left:

Late 1980's: Ray, well into retirement, standing with Dr. Ott in front of EJ Drugs (now Foundation Grounds). Judging by their clothing, and the Santa hat on the pole in front of EJ's, it was a relatively mild December day in Maplewood.

*EEEK* -- what's this, you say? I photographed the only visible remains of the infamous Fyler Avenue Bridge. The old wooden bridge was supported on a series of concrete posts spanning River Des Peres. The posts were angled in such a way for the bridge to begin at Fyler Avenue in Southwest St. Louis, curve rather abruptly left, and then end in Maplewood, near the intersection of Piccadilly and Manhattan (near The Piccadilly restaurant).

Ray and Mae at Shoney's restaurant, which was located at the southeast corner of Manchester and Big Bend in the 1980's.

~ ~ ~ ~ ~ ~ ~ ~ ~ ~ ~ ~ ~ ~ ~ ~

Bertha answered the front door, while Mae finished feeding little Wanda. "Good afternoon, ma'am. I wonder if I might have a moment of your time."

The salesman stepped into the living room with what looked like a folded-up card table with an opening in the middle. He folded out the legs, and assembled the baby seat inside the center opening of the table. "Just how old is your baby?"

Mae hesitated. "I'm sorry, but I'm sure we really can't afford…"

"Mae, take a look at Wanda!" Bertha exclaimed, as she held her. Wanda pulled herself around in her grandma's arms, and stared at the table. She began to reach and lunge forward, acting very interested.

"I think the baby's wanting to try it out," said the excited salesman.

As Mae strapped Wanda into the little seat belt, Wanda began to chatter. She pointed all around at the green marble-colored table surrounding her. She pointed to the alphabet letters printed along the edges.

John laid his cigarette down, pulled out his wallet from his back pocket and walked over. "I think she's gonna have to have the table. How much do you want for it?"

The salesman was overjoyed to accept cash payment for the awkward item he'd been schlepping around Maplewood. "Let me write up a receipt for you, and I'll be on my way!"

"Thanks, Dad and Mom! I can't wait for Ray and Chuck to see her in this."

~ ~ ~ ~ ~ ~ ~ ~ ~ ~ ~ ~ ~ ~ ~ ~ ~ ~

Chuck and Grandma Louise came to visit Mae and Wanda just a few days later. Louise came bearing the gift of a little toy piano.

"Oh, thank you, Louise," exclaimed Mae. "Her very first musical instrument. We'll have to get some photos."

Chuck was very busy these days. He had taken on many of Mae's music store duties after school, since Mae was home most of the time with the new baby. He didn't mind hanging out with Uncle Ray, and making a pretty good salary in comparison to most of his school friends - a whopping 25c an hour. Eleven years older than Wanda, Chuck enjoyed every minute he had with his baby cousin.

After Chuck showed Wanda the way the keys moved on the toy piano, he lifted Wanda onto his knee, and felt a very squishy diaper. "Good gravy, Aunt Mae — I think she needs a change."

"Sorry, Chuck," Mae said, as she took Wanda back to the bedroom. When Wanda was cleaned up, Chuck asked to play with her in the back bedroom, and his Aunt Mae welcomed a little reprieve. She and Louise sat down for a little chat.

"Mae," said Louise, "I'll have to say, we miss you at the music store, but I truly admire the wonderful care you are giving little Wanda. You have always been a hard worker, and you are now also a very caring mother."

"Thank you, Louise." Mae was grateful for Louise's kind comment. There were more and more moments like this, when the two women sensed they were forming a bond. They were each, in their own way, fiercely devoted to, and protective of, those they loved.

Ray began to feel like a fish out of water in the cramped little apartment on Lyndover. He didn't object too strongly when Mae insisted she take Wanda to her parents' house for occasional overnight stays. After all, he had always required a fair amount of sleep, and *someone* needed to get up early in the morning to open the store. Mae wasn't quite sure what to think about this, but her mother explained to her that, since Ray was an "older gentleman" he had lived a lot of years without children — and some attitudes in a husband just aren't worth trying to change.

Ray also found himself missing the days of playing his trumpet around town. He was determined to pick up his trumpet if it only meant rehearsing a bit with his old musician buddies. But times were changing and so was the music. Dance bands that played the type of music Ray grew up playing, just didn't seem to as popular. The fun he used to have leading and performing at the old Maplewood Brownsom Hotel was now just a distant memory.

# CHAPTER 9
## My Special Angel *(Jimmy Duncan)*

### 1957

Mae had just finished the pineapple upside-down cake. She brushed Wanda's hair and smoothed her dress and petticoat as the cake cooled. She changed Buster's diaper once again before leaving.

"Wanda, it's time to see your cousins." She lifted her newborn son Ray Jr., took hold of her daughter's hand, and walked toward the door of their larger, second-story apartment at 2516a Bellevue.

Chuck was already waiting on the other side of the door. He stepped inside as she opened it. "I'll grab the cake, Aunt Mae." He helped his 3-year-old cousin all the way down to Louise's apartment. "Peggy's just gonna love this cake, and holding little Buster again!"

"Chuck, it's been so fun these weeks with Peggy in town. I'm going to miss her, and I know Wanda will, too."

They rang the bell and the door opened. "Hi, Aunt Mae!" There was no mistaking Peggy's soft Texas accent.

"Hi, Peggy," exclaimed Mae as she grabbed and hugged Chuck's sister, "I just love your new dress and shoes. I swear you look taller than just last week. You're turning into a beautiful young lady."

"Aw, I'm not *that* much older than my last visit, Aunt Mae — but my momma did say, even before school started, that I'm growing like a weed."

Louise interrupted."Come on in to the kitchen, Mae, and Chuck can cut some slices of the cake for us. *Chuck*...do be careful..."

Chuck had just lifted Wanda into the air, and was twirling her around in the living room. She giggled. "Yes, Grandma — I'm coming now," said Chuck as he gently placed Wanda back down on the floor.. Wanda walked over and picked up the big sock monkey her grandma kept for her in her apartment, and stuck her thumb in her mouth. Chuck lifted her back up again and smoothed her dress, as he walked into the kitchen. "Do you think I should go get Dad?"

"No, honey. I think we shouldn't wait for him," said Louise. "He said he'd be over a little later. Let's go ahead and have the birthday cake now."

They all came into Grandma Louise's tiny kitchen and found chairs around the table.

"Now Wanda, how many candles do you see?" asked Chuck.

No answer.

"C'mon now, Wanda, sweetie — how many candles?"

Still no answer. The thumb wasn't moving from her mouth.

"Peggy, I *know* she can say it. She helped me count my baseball cards just the other day."

"Now Chuck, you just have to have patience — she'll say it when she's ready." Peggy knew this from experiences with Skip when he was younger.

Chuck did the honors of cutting the cake. Everyone dug in right away; Mae's pineapple upside down cake was always a hit.

"Little Buster is really cute, Aunt Mae. He's just the way you described over the phone."

"I'm just so glad you're still here to celebrate Wanda's birthday with us, Peggy."

"I'm so glad Daddy convinced Momma to let me come up this year. He told her he would have me take some dance lessons with Miss Robinson. It was a real hoot sticking around after my class and watching Wanda's tap dance and ballet class."

"Peggy, maybe Wanda will sing that new song *Tammy* for you. I'll bet I can get her to do it!"

"That's right, Chuck," said Mae. "Peggy, whatever Chuck asks Wanda to do, she'll usually do it. You probably don't believe this, but I swear she's been singing since she was 9 months old, and it's probably because of Chuck's coaxing."

Louise was happy Mae had chosen to have the lunch downstairs in Louise's apartment. Louise never cooked, but she loved to entertain.

"Okay, you two," Louise addressed the two siblings. "You know Uncle Ray will be expecting you over at the store. Better scoot!"

In Peggy's mind, it was a miracle come true to be in Maplewood at all this summer. A miracle, helped along by her dad suggesting that she take dancing lessons in Maplewood. Mary fondly recalled the many couples' dance classes Tom and Mary had taught together at Kennedy Music. She explained to Paul in no uncertain terms she wanted Peggy to have this opportunity.

"I still don't understand why I can't come down to Alta Loma this summer like usual," said Chuck, as they walked down Bellevue to the music store.

"It's okay, Chuck. We'll have a few more days together before the train ride. Maybe today when you're finished with your work, we can ask Uncle Ray if we can make more signs down in the store basement!"

They opened the door to the store. Ray called out with joy. "Hey, Peg Leg! Did y'all have a good time at the birthday party?"

"We sure did, Uncle Ray. I've had so much fun with Wanda and Buster on this trip. Wanda's becoming quite the ballerina!"

"Uncle Ray, how much more needs to be done on the records?" asked Chuck. Since Elvis had just appeared on the Ed Sullivan Show, it was time to rearrange things.

"I'd say you'd better make a stack of those Elvis 78's you left on the floor of the back studio. I know it's fun for the

109

two of you to play with them, but you just can't leave them all spread out like that."

"Peggy's wanting to make more signs," said Chuck.

"You know about the hectograph supplies back near the sink. But preparing the gel and ink can be a real mess. You'll have to clean up."

"No, no — we're thinking about using the new mimeograph machine in the basement that you and Aunt Mae use to make the recital programs. Could we type up a few stencils?"

"Okay, I guess. We just filled the ink drum after the last recital."

"Thanks, Uncle Ray." Both kids made their way to the back studio.

They finished packing up the old 78 records for the storage room. 78 records often didn't hold more than one song per side. For this reason, several single 78's were packaged together in sturdy, thick boxes called "albums." The newer 33 rpm records contained about 6 songs per side, and so they became a newer type of record album, all contained on one disc. For Chuck, the best feature of the new 33's was their flexibility, which prevented them from shattering like the old shellac 78's. He also liked the artsy, colorful cardboard covers.

Peggy and Chuck spent the rest of the afternoon and early evening carefully typing up an ad sign for Elvis' recently released 45 record hits *Heartbreak Hotel*, *Teddy Bear* and *All Shook Up*, cranking out mimeograph copies and distributing them around the City Limits Loop.

The two teenagers went across to the grocery, walked into the Maplewood show to see the signs for the upcoming features, and then walked a little farther west with their posters to Laykem Jewelers. They travelled a little further to The Footlong, resisting the temptation to order a hotdog before dinner. They crossed Manchester to the north side of the street and visited the McCoy family at the diner. Finally, they took a break at Velvet Freeze and cooled off with a Coke. They'd take more posters around tomorrow. They talked and talked — but Chuck noticed they didn't talk much about Texas.

"I'm sure looking forward to high school. Pretty soon we'll be on our own," Peggy mused. "Are you still thinking about becoming a minister or something?"

"No, not exactly. But Grandma Louise and I were talking about me going to St. Louis Bible College. I want to keep learning music, and maybe work as a photographer along with Dad. He often gets calls for those publicity photo shoots."

"I still don't know what I'm gonna do. The thing I love to do the most is travel and see new places. Whenever momma and I can, we drive down to Galveston, or take a little trip somewhere." She sighed. "Paul doesn't let us go that often, though."

"Peg, let's promise each other we'll be together forever. After we're finally done with school, we'll be able to get jobs, and then we'll afford a place of our very own — wherever we choose to live. And we'll visit Mother and Dad and Grandma Louise, whenever *we* decide."

It was time to head back and join the family at Kennedy Music. Peggy took her time because she loved walking around the stores at the City Limits Loop. In those days, Maplewood was still paving over the remaining sections of streetcar rails. The busses continued to circle the Loop near the music store on their way back into the City. The red and white busses would service the City, and the green and white busses would service Maplewood and the County. Exhaust smells abounded, and all of these sights, sounds and smells were associated with being with Chuck in Maplewood and in the music store. Peggy would wrap them up in her memory and carry them back with her to Texas.

When the two teenagers made it back to Kennedy Music, they noticed their dad had arrived. They each gave him a big hug.

Chuck remembered something. "Hey, Dad — why did you used to be called Buster?"

Tom replied: "Your Grandma Louise could certainly explain it better, but I'll try. I was a very little boy when we lived in Glasgow, and I was forever getting into things and hurting myself. One day, while my dad and mom were working in the Kennedy Variety Store, Mom — your Grandma Louise — happened to stroll outside to get a breath of fresh air. She looked across from the town square, and guess what she saw? Me — walking across the second story roof of the Trigg Theatre. I don't even remember how I got up there."

Ray laughed. "Yep, Tom — I remember that day. Mom practically had a heart attack. She kept her cool and coaxed you to slowly find your way back to the fire escape. The Glasgow police were holding their breath, too!"

Peggy chimed in. "Uncle Ray," (Ray noticed her soft Texan drawl), "then why is Ray Jr. nicknamed Buster?"

Tom jumped in to answer his daughter. "That's because Mae says he's a big bruiser, and he's already rolling over and bumping into things. I told her my old nickname would be perfect for Ray Jr. I'll just bet you he'll be ready to bust out of his playpen by the time he's walking, just like I did."

"Okay, everyone — time to close up shop. I'll go get the car so I can drive Mom, Mae, Wanda and Buster over to McCoy's Restaurant. Chuck and Peggy, maybe you can ask Walter McCoy to prepare a couple of tables. Tom, will you and Lee meet us there?"

"Yes — my car is just outside. I'll drive on home to pick up Lee and Paul Gene."

Ray grinned. "We'll have a *big* birthday dinner for Wanda. After all, you only turn three years old once!"

~ ~ ~ ~ ~ ~ ~ ~ ~ ~ ~ ~ ~ ~ ~ ~

The next morning, a tearful Peggy got into her dad's Plymouth. Chuck was a little too angry and sad to come along. He watched them leave from a window.

Tom drove his daughter to Union Station and purchased her ticket back to Houston. Right before she boarded the train, Tom and Peggy gave each other a long embrace. Tom leaned into Peggy's thick, dark curls just one last time. And Peggy always looked forward to Daddy's kiss on her forehead.

"Give your momma my love," Tom called out, as she started up the steps.

Peggy turned and smiled as she brushed away a tear. "I will, Pop."

Tom walked back to the car, teary-eyed himself. The drive back to Maplewood seemed especially painful. Lee, his new wife, along with her son Paul Gene, and Chuck, were holding off on dinner until his return.

Into the evening Tom continued to wonder why things had to be so different this summer for Chuck and Peggy. He picked up the phone.

Paul answered, "Yes…"

"Hi, Paul. Mary there?"

Paul, gruffly yelled out, "MARY...get the phone." Tom was glad Mary hadn't yet gone to bed.

"Hi, Tom. How are you? How was the visit?"

"Fine, fine. Peggy should be arriving about 4:00 am. Mary, I've been meaning to ask you about the arrangement this summer."

Mary hesitated. She spoke quietly. "Tom...I spoke with Paul, and he really thinks its best, this year at least, that Chuck not come."

"Why is that?" Tom tried to get an answer. In the background, he heard Paul:

*"You don't need to explain anything, Mary. We've made up our minds. That's that."*

Mary, changing the subject abruptly, "So Tom, how are you and Lee doing?"

"When you come up sometime to visit Chuck this year, you'll need to meet her. We're getting along great. Did Mae tell you how we met?"

"No."

"Lee works upstairs over Kennedy Music — at the bow factory. We really seemed to hit it off from the start."

Tom paused, then continued. "It's been hard the last few years, Mary. We all thought a year ago that you and Skipper might stay in Maplewood. I don't know how you and Paul are getting on, but Ray, Mae and Chuck — really all of us — have missed you.

"Tom, I gotta go. Thanks for calling. Give my love to the family." *CLICK.*

~ ~ ~ ~ ~ ~ ~ ~ ~ ~ ~ ~ ~ ~ ~ ~ ~ ~

After Peggy's departure, Chuck had Lee's son, Paul Gene, to bum around with. They spent their Sunday after church on their bikes. One of their favorite places to ride was along River Des Peres under the Fyler bridge, all the way south to where the water flow splits off near Wellington Street. It was a nice, temperate ride all summer long.

Chuck looked forward to the Sunday car rides as well, with Grandma along. On one of these rides, Grandma Louise pointed out a house from the past, 4853 Page Avenue. This was also the house where Chuck's father and uncle were born, and where Chuck's great-grandmother, Annie Bittick, had died. Chuck decided then that his step-mom, Lee, and his new step-brother, Paul Gene, needed to learn more about the Bittick-Kennedy family history.

For the rest of the summer of '57, Chuck worked at the music store, and whiled away his free time either on his bike or at the Maplewood Pool.

And once a week or so, when both parents allowed it, he'd make a long-distance call to Texas.

# CHAPTER 10

## It's Now or Never *(Aaron Schroeder, Wally Gold)*

### 1960

"Oh, sh——- I did it again!! I'll never get the hang of this, Ray."

"Nonsense, Mae. Now put your left foot — no Mae, not your right — your *left* foot on the brake. Good, good! Now ... when we start up again, keep your left foot on the brake, engage the clutch with your right foot, and then when you move the gear shift to first gear, move your right foot to the gas pedal and give it gas. You'll get up this hill in no time."

Mae was a nervous wreck. She'd resisted her whole adult life to learn to drive — but now with three children, and an elderly mother-in-law nearby, she had to get the hang of it.

Mae turned around to check on 6-year-old Wanda in the back seat. She took another look around Art Hill in Forest Park, took a deep breath, and grabbed the wheel. She pushed the clutch pedal again with her right foot, and as the car slowly began to roll backwards, she screeched, "Nnnoooo -- What do I do? What do I do?"

*"RIGHT FOOT ON THE GAS!!* Move it to the gas pedal. Give 'er some gas, Mae!"

Mae gave the old Plymouth some gas, and it suddenly lunged forward, and finally, after several attempts, made it up to level ground.

"Okay." after Mae's great triumph, Ray was ready for the next step. "Now let's go forward *down* the hill."

"Do I have to?" Mae, asking between her teeth, tried to avoid uttering too many swear words around her daughter. She gingerly lifted her left foot off the brake. She engaged the clutch in order to shift to first, but because she let the clutch off a little too quickly, the engine sputtered and died.

"D****t, Ray — what's wrong with this old car? I think it's broken. If I have to do this at all, I think I'd do a whole lot better with an automatic. Helen Anderson said the new Ramblers have push-button gear shifts, and no clutch."

"You just need to learn to relax, Mae. You're gonna get the hang of this one — you'll see. Listen, if Tom can teach Chuck how to drive, you're gonna dang well learn how to drive."

~ ~ ~ ~ ~ ~ ~ ~ ~ ~ ~ ~ ~ ~ ~ ~

Chuck asked to stay late one evening, after Kennedy Music closed, to have a serious talk with his Uncle.

"Uncle Ray, you know I have been a very good and dependable employee over the past several years."

"Yes, Chuck — I would agree."

"You know, Uncle Ray, that when Aunt Mae couldn't work at the store anymore, I was here for you."

"Right, Chuck."

"Uncle Ray — you know I am enrolling in St. Louis Bible College soon. I'm going to need to make more money."

Ray took a breath. "Chuck, we knew this day would come. Your Aunt Mae, your Grandma and I talked about it, and thought about what we could offer you. Our adult clerks and teachers must continue to earn enough to support their families."

"I understand, Uncle Ray. So I guess I'll go ahead and take up Seliga's offer for me to work in the shoe store."

"D'ya mean the shoe store just across the street, next to Goldes?"

"That's the one. Dad found out they were looking for a new clerk."

"At least you'll still be working nearby. We'll miss you in the store, Chuck."

Ray couldn't help but feel a great deal of pride and joy in his nephew. He was certainly more like a son than a nephew. He would miss his companionship in the music store.

~ ~ ~ ~ ~ ~ ~ ~ ~ ~ ~ ~ ~ ~ ~ ~

On his first day at Harold Seliga's shoe store, Chuck was feeling a sense of excitement at the thought of attending college. His plan was to save up his money all summer for St. Louis Baptist College (an extension of Hannibal-LeGrange, later to be known as Missouri Baptist College), located in Tower Grove Baptist Church. And along with starting the new job, tonight was his graduation from Maplewood-Richmond Heights High School. After all of his dad's picture taking, and the family walking back home, he picked up the phone and called his best friend.

"Hey Bob…"

"Hey what…"

"What's the plan for tonight?"

"Let's call up the other guys and we'll make one!"

Bob Winning, Bruce Sherman, Fred Marquard, Ed Bryley, and George Mauer joined Chuck on an all-nighter after the cap and gown ceremony. They started at the bowling alley next to the Esquire Theatre, played some pool, and ate at an all-night restaurant. Since George already owned a car, the others pitched in on his portion of the fun. George liked to flaunt the fact that he could hop in his car whenever he wanted, and go as far away from Maplewood as the gas in the tank allowed.

Next morning, Chuck groggily returned home. He just needed a good day of rest. Surely his new boss would understand. He called him.

"Mr. Seliga, I'm just so sorry, but it was graduation last evening, and, well, I was out rather late celebrating."

"I see — well that explains why you're late. When will I see you this morning?"

"That's the reason I'm calling. I'm really needing to take the day off."

Long pause from Mr. Seliga. "So - it sounds like I'm really needing to find a new clerk, Chuck. You may have your day off, and just don't bother coming back."

It seemed like an eternity until Chuck's dad came back home from his shift. They sat down together and he told Tom what had happened. Tom made a call to his long-term friend and fellow merchant Harold Seliga. He assured him that Chuck was normally very dependable, had been reliable in the music store, and that he wouldn't allow this sort of thing to happen again.

# CHAPTER 11

## My Happiness (*Borney Bergantine, Betty Peterson*)

## 1961

"Why do you *always* have to go out on Tuesday evenings?"

"Well, Mae, why *shouldn't* it be Tuesday evening?  Which night of the week would you prefer I go out?"

Mae couldn't come up with a very compelling argument.  Ray's need for his alone time on Tuesday evenings was just something she had to grow to accept.  Owning a business meant giving up his weekends. Saturdays were long business days.  Sundays were the days when Ray and Mae talked over the latest sales and promotions, preparations for the recitals held at the Maplewood-Richmond Heights High School and the Admiral riverboat, or something as simple as balancing out the cash register.  When Ray brought home the sack of coins, Wanda sat at the kitchen table and helped her parents count pennies, nickels, dimes and

quarters into their corresponding paper rolls. She especially looked forward to the silver dollars and 50c pieces.

Ray had hired some clerks to help fill in during Mae's absence. In recent years Mae was busy at home raising three children. Their son Tommy was born at the beginning of a new decade.

Amazingly, Grandma Louise held her own — having just turned 80 — still working behind the desk at Kennedy Music, entering expenditures and bank deposits by hand into the big ledger book.

Wanda was now attending Valley Elementary School, and the Kennedys moved close to the school onto the nearby street of Marion Court (7603). Before she left for school each morning, Wanda would say to her dad, "Don't forget to buy me a nickel's worth of penny candy!" The candy store she was referring to was located just across from her school in the 7500 block of Woodland. Ray would stop there on the way to the music store, and a nickel's worth was ample candy for all 3 of the kids. By now Wanda was becoming quite the little performer, singing and tap dancing in the Kennedy Music School recitals all around town, along with her big cousin, Chuck.

Four-year-old Ray Jr., "Buster," on the other hand, had already lived up to his nickname. As a toddler he had repeatedly pulled up the panels of his playpen, trying to escape into the freedom of the living room. Mae was constantly putting bandaids on his knees and elbows. One day, Buster found his way toward the basement steps and hit his eyebrow so hard, on the long fall to the bottom, that he needed stitches.

Tommy was Mae's biggest baby (10 lbs 11 oz). His feet turned in a little, and so the doctor ordered up a heavy, metal brace fitted with his baby shoes, to keep his feet turned out while he slept. When he learned to turn over in bed, the brace and shoes would often clank hard enough against the wooden slats of the crib to wake him.

Mae made a point of calling her mother more often these days. Mae and her siblings, Hazel and Joe, were glad their parents had found happiness together over the past several years. As John and Bertha's children had many children of their own, their large backyard on Holly Avenue in North County saw many family picnics. John had had the opportunity to meet and enjoy many of his grandchildren, before he passed away in 1959. Bertha's big house on Holly suddenly seemed too empty.

Mae was deep in thought about her mom while she was finishing the lunch dishes. Suddenly she thought she heard a knock. Mae still had the *shhh — baby's asleep* door hanger on the outside of the front door. She wondered if Wanda and Buster had come around the front from their swing set in the back yard.

*"Hi, Hazel!"* Mae whispered enthusiastically as she tried to let Hazel in as quietly as possible. She was glad to see her mother and Hazel's five children walking up just behind her.

"We thought we'd take a chance. We were in Maplewood anyway, and thought we'd drop by. Is this a good time?"

*"I'm so glad you came. Tommy's still asleep."* Mae tiptoed outside and quietly spoke between two slats of the wooden fence. *"Wanda — Buster — we have visitors."*

Wanda and Ray Jr. came bounding in through the back door, slamming the screen door. Tommy rolled over. *CLUNK.* He immediately awoke from his nap.

Mae laughed loudly. "It's just as well — I wanted you to see how much he's grown. Remember how big he was to begin with?"

"Now you officially have a houseful of kids just like I do! Oh, my — all three of them have grown so much!"

Mae took the big, clunky foot brace off Tommy's feet and placed him into the playpen. Hazel's oldest daughter, Robbie, walked over next to him.

"He's so cute, Aunt Mae. Look at all of that blonde hair."

"And he had that little issue with his eyes too, right Mae?" asked Bertha. "How's he doing with that?"

"The redness and puffiness seem to be gone now. He actually needed to get his tear ducts pierced since they weren't allowing his tears through. I don't think we'll need a refill on the medicated eyedrops. As you heard on the Admiral last Saturday, he cries just fine now!"

Mae put the tea kettle on for some instant coffee. "So what brings all of you to Maplewood today?"

Bertha, her mother, spoke up. "After watching Wanda and Chuck perform, Robbie Sue is interested in signing up for some dance lessons., right Robbie? I can just bring her in to Maplewood on the bus from now on, but on this first trip we thought we'd all come in together."

"I think that's wonderful, Robbie." Mae tested the temperature of Tommy's milk bottle. "Have you met your new dance instructor?"

"Yes," said Hazel, "Louise took us to the dance studio today. Laura Robinson took a moment to talk with us. She said she has several other children in 5th grade in the dance class this year, didn't she, Robbie?"

"It seems just like yesterday," Mae recalled, "that both Chuck and Peggy took dance lessons from Laura."

Bertha noticed Mae's framed photograph of Wanda dancing on the Admiral when she was four years old. "Wanda loves her dance lessons with Miss Laura — right, Wanda?"

"Yes, Grandma."

Bertha decided to have some fun. "I think we'll have to take George Jr. and Ronnie in and sign them up for ballet. Maybe Buster can join them."

"I don't wanna dance, Grandma," said George Jr.

"Your grandma is just joking," said Mae. "You don't need to take dance lessons unless you want to." She turned to Bertha. "How are you doing, Mom?"

"Oh, fine, fine," said Bertha. She sighed. "It's just that the house seems empty."

"Do Joe and Jean come by very often? They don't live too far from you."

"Ruxton Street is a bit of a drive, but Joe and Jean do drop by with their three kids once in awhile." "You know Mae and Hazel, you all are *busy busy busy* with your families. And that's as it should be. The kids are the most important thing. I don't expect any of you to have the time to come by too often."

"Still, I'll bet if you let us help you sell that big old house, you can find a smaller place closer to one of us."

"Joe and I have been encouraging her to do that too, Mae," Hazel interjected.

The kids were squirming. Robbie, the oldest, decided to stay inside and watch Tommy while the other cousins went out back to swing. Mae poured the hot water into the cups, and the ladies helped themselves to the freeze-dried granules. Bertha asked Mae where she kept her Saccharin.

"Now don't you kids be telling me what to do — I'll sell my house when I want to. There are lots of memories in that big old house — our barbecues in the back yard, the old swimming pool and slide for the grandkids... it's close to the downtown bus lines for work, and so I'm doing just fine. I can take care of myself — and I'm not nearly as frail as Mae's mother-in-law. I will have to say though, Mae, she still seems to be quite active. Is she really still living alone?"

"Well, yes and no — Ray and I keep a close eye on her. And I pick her up for church Sunday mornings."

"Church? You're going to church again, Mae?" asked Hazel.

"Since you asked, yes, I am. The Reverend Kellogg is very nice. He baptized me."

"You're no longer Catholic, then?" asked her mother.

"I don't think of it that way, Mom — it's just that Louise and Chuck go to the Baptist Church regularly, and since I often drive them, and want my own kids to attend Sunday School, I've taken on teaching a primary class. Ray would go — but he wants his one full day off from Kennedy Music to just sleep in."

"Hmmm — Mom, church would probably be good for you as well —" interjected Hazel.

127

"Don't tell me what to do, Hazel."

# CHAPTER 12
## Cryin' in the Rain *(Everly Brothers)*

### 1962

The call came in the middle of the night from the Maplewood police. A massive fire had destroyed the 7179 building. Most of the inventory inside Kennedy Music couldn't be salvaged.

Many of the old buildings along Manchester (F. W. Woolworth's, Goldes) still didn't have sprinkler systems. A smoldering cigarette butt in the trash could have disastrous overnight results.

Bleary-eyed and bewildered the next morning, Ray drove down to the store. He stood outside alongside Walter McCoy, whose restaurant was spared from the flames. "Ray, I'm glad we all took out that business insurance. What would you do otherwise?"

Ray looked around - the Brownsom apartment buildings, the Maplewood Theatre - almost every other building in sight - were intact. Kennedy Music enjoyed success at this location for 13 years.

Once again, a potential disaster was averted. A nice, large storefront opened up. It was a more prime location - and ironically, exactly catty-cornered from the Firestone building (their very first location), at Manchester and Marshall. EJ's Drug Store was in the same building. Around the side of the building, closer to Marietta and the old Maplewood Venetian Blinds, they opened a teaching studio.

By the early 1960's baton and dance students had dwindled. Instrumental sales and rentals were still strong. But Kennedy Music was especially known for their records — 45's and 33's — throughout the years they occupied the 7302 Manchester location.

Tom and Lee Kennedy had moved into a house on Anna Avenue, very close to Kennedy Music.

"Ray," Tom phoned his older brother, "I picked up Peggy at Union Station yesterday. She's wanting to spend her entire summer up here, after high school graduation, and has decided to attend St. Louis Baptist College in the fall, just like Chuck."

"That's great, Tom. Is Chuck sticking around this summer?"

"I think so. He'll most likely continue working at Seliga Shoes in Maplewood."

"I'm happy for you, Tom."

~ ~ ~ ~ ~ ~ ~ ~ ~ ~ ~ ~ ~ ~ ~ ~

Peggy came into the store to visit her Uncle Ray the next day.

"Hey, Uncle Raaay!"

"Hi there, Peg-Leg!" They gave each other a bear hug.

"How's your mother?"

"Oh, she's just fine."

"Mae and I sure miss her. D'ya think she might bring Skipper up to visit again?"

Ray didn't want to pry, but he was curious about her quick move in and out of Maplewood a few years back.

Peggy appeared a bit anxious, and then smiled for her uncle's sake. "I've sure been talking to her about coming up here. Chuck and I would love it."

She happily remembered something else. "Guess what, Uncle Ray? Do you remember how much I love cheerleading?"

"Of course."

"Well, I tried and tried to join the squad at school, and I've never been chosen. I just tried out for the SLBC cheerleaders — and just like that, I made the squad!"

"Good for you, Peg Leg! I remember Wanda asking you to show her the different routines over the years. How do you like your job at Citizen's Bank?"

"It's okay. I'm doing some data entry at the bank — it should keep me busy this summer. Speaking of Wanda, how is she? How are the boys?"

"They're doing just great. Wanda's been asking to see you. She's just begun piano lessons right here in the music school, and she really loves it."

"I can't wait to see all three of them!"

~ ~ ~ ~ ~ ~ ~ ~ ~ ~ ~ ~ ~ ~ ~ ~ ~

Toward the end of the summer, Peggy had saved up her money for the first semester, and enrolled at SLBC. As school began, she enjoyed attending the church where Chuck was serving. He sang with a quartet at First Baptist Church in Creve Coeur.

Peggy could no longer work full time at Citizen's Bank when she began her studies. She asked her Uncle Ray for a part-time job at Kennedy Music, and he was glad to bring her on.

One afternoon, as she entered the store, it was obvious Peggy had been crying.

"What's the matter, Peg?"

She didn't want to talk about it. Ray would call his brother that evening.

Peggy really didn't seem like herself, so Ray decided it was an emergency. He called MacDonnell Aircraft, and the telephone operator notified Tom's department. It took a few moments for Tom to get patched in to the call.

"Tom, I think there's something up with Peggy. I think you should take a moment to speak with her."

Tom was only able to speak over the phone briefly, and assured Peggy they would talk that evening. Peggy was able to get through the remainder of her work day without more tears. But upon his arrival home that evening, Tom found Peggy sobbing in her bedroom. Chuck sat next to her.

"What's the matter, honey bunch? You need to talk to me."

"Dad — Chuck — I really don't know how to begin…"

"What do you mean, Peg?" Chuck embraced his sister. "You can tell me anything. You know that."

"If I tell you — you both gotta swear you … you won't kill him."

Suddenly — finally — Peggy came clean.

"It's Paul, our stepdad. Remember, Dad, the year I thought I'd finish at Lyndover School but stayed in Texas after the holidays? And the following summer, when Chuck wanted to come down to Texas, and Momma refused? It wasn't Momma who refused to invite Chuck down — it was Paul."

"What's been going on, Peggy?" Chuck was feeling more than a little anger and suspicion.

"He — he isn't a very good stepdad." Peggy suddenly sat upright on the edge of the bed and wiped her face, speaking with resolution. For the first time in her life, she let go of the secrets she had kept -- year after year of physical and mental abuse she and Skipper had endured.

133

"Dad, Chuck — I will never, ever go down there and subject myself to him again. But I also don't want to leave Momma and Skipper."

Tom immediately walked to the telephone to call Mary.

"Mary? You okay?"
Neither Tom nor Mary concerned themselves with long distance telephone charges as Mary released her many years of pent up frustration and deeply rooted fears. She expressed her guilt, recalling how she had observed terrible things happening at home to both Peggy and Skipper, feeling hopelessly unable to stop it.

"Tom, I'm glad Peggy is up there with all of you. Please tell her to stop worrying about me. I'm so…" she began to cry.

"Take your time, Mary."

I'm just — I just can't do this anymore. Paul has kept a roof over our heads, but I'm afraid to remain here any longer."

"Mary, come up here. We'll find you a job in Maplewood and a place to stay."

Chuck was furious. It had been bad enough his mom and dad had lived apart all those years. He knew Paul was a disciplinarian with Skipper, and even with Chuck from time to time during his visits -- but, after all, they were boys. His mother and his sister *certainly* never deserved harsh treatment. If Chuck had ever been angry enough to really hurt someone, it was now.

"I sure wish you would have told me about him sooner."

Peggy replied, "Do you remember, Chuck, when we were very little, visiting with Uncle Ray at the store, and I was sitting on the counter near the cash register? We were horsing around. You walked past me, like you didn't see me, and then grabbed me by the legs and I fell. Do you remember how stern Uncle Ray's voice was when he scolded you, and how he took me to Dr. Ott to make sure I hadn't broken anything? Well, all I could think of when that happened, was how kind Uncle Ray was to the both of us. He would never dream of really hurting us. None of my friends in Texas had any idea of what was going on at home, and I was too ashamed and scared to tell anyone."

Skipper, now 16 years old, encouraged his mother to leave this time. They left Texas while his father was at work one day. Chuck and Peggy, and all of the Kennedys, welcomed Mary and Skipper back in Maplewood. And Mary never again went back to live with Paul.

After too many years of living apart, Chuck and Peggy, as young adults, were finally free to enjoy each other's companionship, whenever they pleased.

And Peggy began a long process of healing.

# CHAPTER 13

## 'Where Have All the Flowers Gone' *(Pete Seeger and Joe Hickerson)*

### 1963

In spite of the wear and tear of 82 years, Louise Kennedy held her own. She continued to sit at her desk at Kennedy Music several hours a week. Ray and Mae asked to see the music studio appointment book from time to time, even though Louise swore she kept it correctly. Students walked into the store to check in for their weekly lesson. They would then walk around the corner to the studio to meet their instructor in the music studio. Occasionally there was no instructor scheduled at that particular time, and other times Louise forgot that another student was scheduled for the same time with the same instructor.

Mae suggested to Ray that they needed to find a larger place to live, since the small house on Marion Court didn't have an extra bedroom for Louise. So Ray, Mae and their children invited Grandma Louise to live with them at 7394 Maple, a 4-bedroom, 2-story house with a basement. It was two doors down from the old Maplewood Loop on Sutton, directly across from the Cape Harper Building.

Grandma Louise realized she hadn't been particularly attentive to her granddaughter over the many half-summers Peggy had visited Maplewood. Peggy had never felt Grandma Louise was particularly friendly toward her. Chuck, on the other hand, had always been the apple of her eye. Louise had promised Tom she would take good care of Chuck in his absence. She had grown to love Chuck's companionship. Louise felt a bit jealous of the closeness Chuck and Peggy shared while they were children. Now that Chuck was on his own and Peggy was working in the store, Louise began to notice this beautiful, soft spoken, kind, Christian young lady. Peggy showed her aging grandmother grace and consideration. Louise often told her stories of earlier days, while walking slow, easy paces together along Marshall Avenue each evening, on their way home from Kennedy Music.

~ ~ ~ ~ ~ ~ ~ ~ ~ ~ ~ ~ ~ ~ ~ ~

"Hello…"

"Grandma, it's Chuck. How are you doing?"

"Oh, fine, fine! How good to hear from you, Chuck. How are your studies?"

"Grandma, I have a surprise to tell you. I wanted you to be the very first person to know. Do you remember meeting Judi?"

"Judi...oh, yes — *yes*. She's that nice young girl I met this summer. You wrote a song about her and played it for all of us, remember?"

"Well, Grandma — brace yourself — we're married."

Long silence.

"Grandma, are you okay?"

Neither Chuck nor Judi had the means with which to throw a big reception, and rather than ask their parents, they decided to elope. About a month and a half later, Chuck decided to tell his grandma. Of course, as soon as Grandma Louise knew, the word was out in Maplewood, and the entire Kennedy family was overjoyed. They welcomed Judi into the family with open arms. Grandma Louise, honored that she was the first to know about the marriage, purchased the young couple a nice full set of bedroom furniture.

The couple decided to move to Liberty, Missouri for Spring semester, so Chuck could continue his music and ministry studies at William Jewell College near Kansas City. In mid-November, he and Judi decided to pay another visit to their Uncle Ray at the music store. They were also looking forward to one more Thanksgiving dinner at Aunt George's house.

After class he went to the school cafe, and just as he was about to drop a dime into the pay phone, he noticed a crowd of students surrounding the small Admiral TV set. The meaning of the words being spoken over the airwaves were processing in Chuck's mind as if they had been spoken in slow motion. It was Walter Cronkite:

*"An electrifying flash came over the wires — that bullet shots had been heard to ring out in the Kennedy motorcade. There is the report in Dallas that the President is dead, but that has not been confirmed by any other source..."*

Back in Maplewood, Wanda was sitting in Mrs. Robinson's 3rd-grade class at Valley Elementary School, when the principle began to announce the horrific news:

*"I regret to inform you, that President Kennedy was shot…and killed today."*

Immediately, Wanda raised the top of her desk, and laid her head down on top of the books inside. Tears came to her eyes. Her last name was the same as the President of the United States, and she suddenly felt fearful and vulnerable.

For many, the raw uncertainty experienced during these events would subside over time, but never entirely disappear.

Chuck was drawn, even more strongly, back to Kennedy Music for a visit. As he sat and watched Ray finish up with his customer, demonstrating the full sound of the Gibson 12-string, he thought perhaps the years might be adding a bit of wear and tear to his Uncle's face. But the years certainly weren't slowing him down. Ray was still a very convincing salesman. As he sat and waited, Chuck sensed a deepening desire to follow God's Call, even if it meant serving Him far away from his hometown. At the same time, he breathed a silent prayer that his family in Maplewood — his grandmother, Aunt George, father, sister and brother, Uncle Ray, Aunt Mae, and three young cousins — would always remain safe and sound.

Chuck's Uncle Ray was never very outspoken when it came to matters of his faith, but his relationships with others clearly and consistently demonstrated the deep-rooted faith of his childhood. Ray was always greeted by someone as he walked up and down Manchester Avenue. He was never too busy for a bit of impromptu conversation. He seemed to know and get along with everyone. He hardly ever lost his temper. Chuck never saw him curse or swear in public. He could smoke one cigarette in an evening, or perhaps drink one beer when he went out with a friend. "Everything in moderation" was Ray's motto. He treated all of his music store customers with courtesy and respect. Ray had been asked at one point whether he would consider running for city government, but he declined. Although a part of him loved the thought of taking on the challenge, Ray devoted himself to the family business, his mother, his brother, his wife and his children.

When Chuck observed his Uncle Ray these days, and the choices he had made over the years, he realized Ray had become his role model in more ways than one. And Chuck was proud of his Uncle Ray.

Chuck attended William Jewell College for two years, 1963-1965. During his last year at Jewell, he and Judi became proud first-time parents of a son — Charles Raymond Kennedy Jr.

# CHAPTER 14
## I Want to Hold Your Hand *(The Beatles)*

### 1964

One of the opportunities music stores had in the 60's, was to host record signings for the many regional rock bands that were receiving promotion from the recording labels. The Intruders was one such band.

"Whatever happened to good music?" Ray would say when these bands came to town. His young sons would agree. Still, it was a great chance to fill the store with people, and to sell lots of 45's.

On the day of their visit, Ray played their single, *Total Raunch*, over the outside stereo speakers. Grandma Louise decided this would be the day she would leave the music store a little early. Ray's brother Tom was there to take publicity photos.    Ray introduced and interviewed the Intruders for a store packed with excited teenagers.    Mae put little Tommy on top of Ray's shoulders so he wouldn't get lost in the shuffle. After the interview, Ray Jr. helped his dad with the "serious" customers across the aisle looking at guitars, drums and amplifiers, while Wanda helped watch Tommy behind the counter, and Mae completed the last few record sales.    At the end of a very hectic Saturday afternoon, Mae kicked off her shoes and sat down on the stool behind the counter.    She overheard a bit of loud talking across the room, and glanced over at Ray and Ray Jr.

"Whad'ya mean he can tune it?  He's just a kid!  I didn't come all the way back here to have a *kid* tune my guitar..."

This made Ray all the more determined for his son to tune that beautiful 12-string Martin guitar, which the customer had purchased earlier in the week.  He hadn't had time to get it tuned Monday, so Ray had said to come back Saturday  -- and no one was going to tell Ray that his son, who had perfect pitch, didn't have the ability to tune a guitar.

He leaned over and said quietly, "Just take your time, Buster."  After a few minutes, Ray Jr. double-checked the octave strings, strummed a few E chords, and handed the guitar back to the customer.

"Well, I'll be --" said the man, and he took the guitar and left.

Just before locking up, Ray saw Peggy walking in, arm in arm with a surprise guest.

"Daddy — Uncle Ray — I want you to meet Troy."

Troy Clenney reached out his hand to Peggy's dad and uncle.  While still at SLBC a couple years ago, Chuck had introduced Peggy to his very good friend and classmate.  Peggy was instantly attracted to Troy's gentle strength, but a dating relationship, up until now, had been something she avoided. Chuck certainly understood her reluctance. However, over a period of time she began to feel the courage to get to know Troy better.

"What brings you to Maplewood, Troy?" asked Tom.

"Chuck gave me a call. He just finalized things at the Maplewood Baptist Church. Our Revival team will be leading all next week, Monday through Friday evening. I sure hope all of you attend. I will be giving what we call a Chalk Talk on Wednesday evening."

"I'll make a point of it," said Tom. "I'll bet the two of you make a good team. I'll also invite Lee and Paul Gene when I get home."

Louise, Ray, Mae, Tom, Lee, Mary, Peggy and Ray's three children filled a church pew that Wednesday. They sang along as Chuck led the old hymns, and then watched and listened as Troy used a chalkboard and a few small pieces of chalk to create an intriguing portrait of Jesus, as he shared the gospel message. After the service, his large, gentle hand held Peggy's hand affectionately as they talked with the Kennedys.

Troy had come to St. Louis from his family's farm in Troy, Illinois. He had never left home as a child and had no desire to travel. Peggy, on the other hand, jumped at any excuse to go anywhere and everywhere. She told everyone the story of their first Greyhound bus trip together from St. Louis to Liberty, Missouri, to visit Chuck and Judi.

"The bus driver told us we would take a half-hour lunch break. The people all filed off, and Troy was the last person sitting on the bus. I thought he was following right behind me, but he wasn't. When it didn't look like Troy was getting up, the bus driver walked back and talked with him. Troy told the driver he just wanted to stay in his seat," Peggy lovingly pulled him close as she spoke, "but the bus driver insisted that he exit the bus. I think Troy was just a little scared since he was in a new town, that he might get lost and miss the bus. I told him he needn't worry, that I'd never let him out of my sight that long!"

143

Tom, Mary and Chuck all smiled. Mary, in particular, was overjoyed Peggy had found someone who cherished her so deeply.

~ ~ ~ ~ ~ ~ ~ ~ ~ ~ ~ ~ ~ ~ ~ ~ ~

That summer, Peggy and Troy were married at the Maplewood Baptist Church. Peggy's little cousin Ray Jr. was their ring bearer, and Grandma Louise was proud to have her picture taken with the happy couple.

# CHAPTER 15
## Blowin' in the Wind *(Bob Dylan)*

### 1966

It was another one of those middle-of-the-night scares, and this time the face of the Maplewood business district was changed forever. The smoke smell seemed to hang in the air for hours, disturbing everyone's sleep. Goldes Department Store had burned to the ground.

Maplewood had always been home to small, specialty stores, which drew people in from neighboring areas for their unique offerings (Worths, Nacy's, Thom McAnn Shoes). There were also several larger anchor-type stores, such as Sears, Newberry's, Katz Drugs and Woolworth's.

Originating in St. Louis in 1925, the Goldes chain of eight stores were known as "junior" department stores. They didn't carry huge items such as refrigerators or kitchen ranges, but they did stock a wide variety of quality goods. Their many loyal customers recommended Goldes to their friends because of the personalized service. For instance, if you purchased a dress at Goldes, they provided custom fitting and alterations. "If you look good we look good" became their motto.

The north side of the 7300 block of Manchester had basically been known as the Goldes side of Manchester, since Goldes spanned a width equal to at least three of Maplewood's larger storefronts. Goldes had originally been hesitant to build on the north side of the block, but their loyal customers were fine with crossing the street from the more frequented south side. So after the fire, there a huge, painfully gaping hole, smack in the middle of Maplewood.

The owners of Goldes decided not to rebuild. For a while, they offered free bus rides up to their Hazelwood store to their Maplewood customers. For what seemed to be an eternity, the open lot on the north side of Manchester remained barricaded, and many solutions were proposed.

Maplewood had not yet felt the full impact of this particular change in its retail landscape, and Ray and Mae persevered. Kennedy Music continued to be known as Maplewood's only full-service music store, and had a strong reputation as an instrument, record and sheet music provider throughout the surrounding counties.

~ ~ ~ ~ ~ ~ ~ ~ ~ ~ ~ ~ ~ ~ ~ ~

"CH — CH — HMMM. . ." Six-year-old Tommy sat on the the living room floor with his legs crossed. He would play this game a lot — pretending to be a record player. As Tommy said "CH" he stiffly moved his right forearm up. On the second "CH" he moved his forearm to the left a bit. On the "HMMM" he dropped the "needle," his pointer finger, onto the "record" on his lap. This time, he acted like he was playing "Swinging Shepherd Blues." Other times he'd grunt out the bass line as he remembered the recordings of Ray Brown from the many times his dad and older brother had played the recordings.

Meanwhile, Mae was dipping the long wallpaper strips into the bucket of wet glue, stepping up from the paint tarp onto the step ladder, and carefully smoothing the soggy paper onto the new music room walls. Large, older homes customarily had dining room furniture, but not the new Kennedy home. The dining room at 7320 Vine Street had an upright Ballwin Acrosonic piano, a record player and a variety of musical instruments. Mae preferred it this way, content listening to her children playing music or singing in the next room while she served simple, family-style meals in the kitchen. When she wasn't chauffeuring her children to and from music lessons, or working on the sheet music inventory at the music store, Mae spruced up and decorated their new home on Vine Street. She took great pride in this house. It was the only building in Maplewood, or anywhere, that Ray and Mae ever owned.

Nine-year-old Ray Jr. found a friend on Maple Avenue. Tom Wilson was a tall man with long, thick fingers, who played the piano at Shakey's Pizza Parlor on Big Bend. Tom Wilson also happened to be a friend and colleague of Ray, during the Brownsom Hotel big band days. Tom Wilson played with a very quick, entertaining stride-bass left hand, which reminded Ray a little of Art Tatum. Ray Jr. would often ask his dad if they could drive over and order a pizza at Shakey's just so they could sit together and listen a while. And when Ray Jr. learned Tom's work schedule, he would walk over and wait on the steps of Tom's apartment building, so that his new friend could teach him how to play that stride bass piano style.

It was Saturday morning. Twelve-year-old Wanda walked from the store to the Maplewood Post Office with the mail box key. While walking back, she decided she would stop in and finish signing paperwork for her new savings account — her dad and mom were good friends with the people at Citizens Bank. Wanda enjoyed showing off her new passbook, and her shiny-new gold-colored bank pen. She felt very grown up.

"Good for you, Wanda," her dad replied. "You'll earn 5% on your salary, and it'll be safe in the bank."

Ray walked back to Louise's desk and opened the mail that Wanda had just brought to them. Both Ray and Wanda couldn't help but notice Louise's shakiness. "Mom, are you sure you don't want Wanda to finish those journal entries for you?"

"No thank you, Ray," replied Louise. Her voice was weak from age, and her speech was a bit shaky and slow. "But if you begin to notice errors, you be sure and let me know." It was hard to decipher Louise's handwriting at all, but no one had the heart to press the issue.

Ray tore open another envelope. He looked up with a grin. "Wanda ... I have a surprise for you ..."

He held up the two tickets. Wanda walked over. She had been glancing through the new 45 records.

"Ohhh, Dad!"

Ray knew Wanda would hardly be able to contain herself — these were tickets to the Beatles concert August 21,1966, at the recently-built Busch Stadium.

"That's your brother Tommy's birthday. Do you think we maybe should give the tickets to him and Buster?"

Ray laughed. They had kept this treat for Wanda a secret. The tickets, marked $5.50, were distributed by Stix, Baer and Fuller to the record stores around town for promotional purposes.

"Tommy and Buster would hate it," Wanda replied. "They don't listen to the Beatles."

"That's for sure," Ray replied. "Remember when we made them come along to the Maplewood Theatre to see *A Hard Day's Night?* That movie was about the biggest bunch of nothing I ever saw."

"Dad, you and the boys just don't get it."

"Who do you think you'll invite to go with you to the concert?" asked Louise.

"I guess I'll ask Mom."

Ray interjected. "After that disgusting album cover, we'll see how many people show up for that concert."

Ray was referring to the Yesterday and Today album, recently released in June, 1966. "I can still remember Mae's expression when she unpacked the box."

Upon ripping open the first album box and inspecting the first record jacket — the photo of four Beatles smiling in white lab coats, seemingly oblivious to the bloody cuts of meat and plastic baby doll heads strewn about them. Mae had absolutely refused to sell the album in the music store. Kennedy Music wasn't the only store to return the Beatles' butcher album to Capitol Records.

"Dad, you and Mom shouldn't be so uptight. You should feel way more uptight over the Vietnam War than over that record jacket." The Beatles could do no wrong in Wanda's eyes.

Wanda was now attending Lyndover Junior High School. By 1966 she had studied the piano for five years. As a break from homework, and

149

from scales, Bach Preludes and Chopin waltzes, she'd walk over to the music room stereo system, carefully lay the phonograph needle on the latest Beatles album, and turn off all the lights. She'd sit against the wall, tune out the sound of dishes in the kitchen, and dream of traveling to Liverpool to meet and marry Paul McCartney.

Wanda had progressed quickly through the ranks of the Kennedy music school piano instructors. She was now studying at the St. Louis Institute of Music, located in Clayton. Grandmother Louise had been her first teacher, and she had high hopes Wanda would follow in Chuck's footsteps to become a church musician. "You should also learn to play the organ, Wanda — it will be a good skill to have someday!" But Wanda wouldn't hear of it. Piano was her instrument.

Ray Jr. was in the fourth grade at Valley Elementary. He would constantly ask his dad to order artists such as Miles Davis, John Coltrane and Freddy Hubbard. He made lists of his choices out of the huge Phonolog book. The Phonolog contained listings of all available recordings from the major labels. Its pages were regularly updated and then mailed to the record stores. The pages came pre-punched so they could be inserted into the specially-made binder, and the book was kept propped open for reference on top of an accessible cabinet.

Tommy followed his older brother's lead. While so many of their school friends were preoccupied with British rock and roll, Ray's two sons borrowed musical instruments from the store, and did their best from year to year to emulate Maynard Ferguson's screaming trumpet double-high C's, Charlie Mingus' bass lines, and Oscar Peterson's piano style.

# CHAPTER 16
## Music Music Music *(Stephen Weiss and Bernie Baum)*

### 1968

All three of Ray and Mae's children lived and breathed music, just like their parents. Both Ray and Mae looked for ways to develop their talents.

Mae took Wanda regularly to St. Louis Symphony performances, and mother and daughter reserved box seats every summer at the St. Louis Municipal Opera. At age 14 Wanda had set her eyes on the Juilliard School in New York City, and a career as a concert pianist. At the same time, she loved listening to Jean Hartin play hymns on Sunday morning close to home at Maplewood Baptist Church. There was something about Jean's stylistic renditions that brought old church hymns to life. Jean, along with Bill Stillwell, who had a wonderfully powerful tenor voice, served as the youth choir director Wednesday evenings. Wanda always had her homework finished early on Wednesdays, and unless she had a raging fever, Ray and Mae planned on her taking off work at Kennedy Music early enough to walk around the corner for the Wednesday evening church supper, youth choir rehearsal and church prayer meeting.

Ray had heard of Herb Drury. He went to hear Herb at Schneidhorst's Restaurant, where he was performing with his jazz trio — Jerry Cherry on upright bass and Art Heigel on drums. He and Mae then decided it would be fun to bring the kids to hear the trio at the Chase Park Plaza the following weekend.

The boys dressed up in their finest, and so did Wanda. The three kids sat in the back seat of the family station wagon, with Wanda in the middle. As usual, the two boys would talk across her about the latest jazz recordings they had heard. Annoyed, she'd often poke one of them.

"Stop it, Wanda!" Tommy would say.

"Knock it off, Wanda!" Ray Jr. would echo.

"Boys, leave your sister alone. Be nice to her."

The family enjoyed a very special night at the Chase, eating fancy food and listening to the best jazz trio in the St. Louis area.

"Boys, try to fold your napkins neatly before laying them next to your plate." The waiter handed Ray the bill. Ray reached into his pocket. "Wow, forty dollars…hmmm…Mae, d'ya have some cash?" Ray had known the Tenderloin Room steaks at the Chase would be a bit pricier than the Toll House steaks in Maplewood, but then again, Ray was typically a bit short when it came to leaving a tip, in spite of Mae's reminders.

Ray also had a friend in town named Frank Riehl — Frank had a studio on Hampton Avenue in South St. Louis where he taught music and chord theory.

Both Herb Drury and Frank Riehl were impressed with Ray Jr.'s innate ear for jazz improvisation. Frank helped Ray Jr. build on his natural understanding of keyboard harmony. Herb mentored Ray Jr. in many ways — not only with his sophisticated piano stylings, but also as a lifelong student of the instrument. Herb instilled the love of music into the many students he taught.

Tommy kept contact with Herb Drury's bass player, Jerry Cherry. He was mesmerized by Jerry's ease with the instrument. Jerry took Tommy under his wing, imparting his unique knowledge of the instrument. Tommy yearned for the day he might have a double bass of his very own.

# CHAPTER 17
## Reflections of my Life *(The Marmalade)*

### 1970

It was apparent in the early part of 1970 that Louise was going downhill physically. She was now 87 years old, and when Louise's frailty made it no longer possible for her to live at home comfortably, Aunt George encouraged Louise's sons to place her in a nursing home. After all, Aunt George said, "Ray and Mae have enough on their plates caring for those children and working at the music store."

Mae thought about the powerful influence Louise had had on her family. Certainly, Mae and Louise had butted heads numerous times, but they also held one another in very high esteem.

Throughout their marriage, Mae and Ray had talked openly and honestly. Re-evaluating his life, while visiting his mother in the nursing home, Ray realized that the daily responsibilities of running a music store and school had over the years supplanted his desire to develop a performing career. After all, his mother had always encouraged him to settle down and live a respectable life. Mae reminded Ray that everyone has to make choices — very few, if any, can accomplish everything they set out to do. Both Louise and Mae had a great deal of respect for the choices Ray had made over the years to love and support his family.

But Mae also wanted her two sons, and her daughter, to reach for more.

In April of 1970, Louise peacefully passed away at Chastain Nursing home. Wanda and Mae helped fulfill Ray's duties in the music store that week, as he and his brother Tom took time to grieve the loss of their mother.

~ ~ ~ ~ ~ ~ ~ ~ ~ ~ ~ ~ ~ ~ ~ ~ ~

Over the next few years, Golmans and P.N. Hirsch each in turn occupied the old Goldes space, but neither remained very long. In the past, shoppers were accustomed to finding everything within easy walking distance. The newer trend beginning in the 1970's were sprawling, climate-controlled malls, accessible both by car and bus. This changing retail landscape meant smaller populations like Maplewood couldn't possibly compete. Many of the older businesses and professionals contemplated whether they wanted to relocate into a mall or more affluent neighborhood, or whether it was simply time to retire.

As shopping trends changed, so did perceptions of retail appearance. For Maplewood, which would be more cost effective — to repair and maintain, or to tear down and build new?

Something had to be done if Maplewood was to continue to grow. Business owners and local government leaders discussed the issue. Under the leadership of Mayor Josef Hammes, Maplewood was to be "revitalized."

Mae returned home one evening late, after a Maplewood Chamber of Commerce meeting. "I sure hope the new plan is successful. They're drawing up a blueprint for the new Maplewood Municipal Parking Garage. Eddie's Lounge, where the Chamber has been meeting, will be torn down. Arthur Avenue residents will need to relocate."

The plan was to build a new Kmart store toward the back of a two-level parking garage. New storefronts would be integrated into the front of the garage at street level, facing Manchester.

"What about the south side of the street?" asked Ray, hoping they wouldn't need to move yet again.

"Victor Kintz next door at the pharmacy asked that very same question tonight. For now it looks like EJ's and Kennedy Music will stay put."

~ ~ ~ ~ ~ ~ ~ ~ ~ ~ ~ ~ ~ ~ ~

Ray Jr. had just begun high school. He played trumpet in the Maplewood-Richmond Heights High School marching band, where he met Paul Stephens and Brian Ottolini. A handful of students in the 9th grade shared Ray's interest in the famous trumpet player, Maynard Ferguson. The MRH band director, Jean Chard, became Ray's favorite teacher, and had also met Ray's brother Tommy during a Meet the Teacher night.

One day, Mae and Ray Jr. drove up to Lyndover Junior High to pick up Tommy. They had a surprise for him — laying across the inside of the red Rambler station wagon, from the front passenger seat all the way to the rear window, was a double bass.

"Wow, Buss — this is the bass we saw at the high school. How'd you get this?"

"Mr. Chard spoke with the orchestra director, John Dolan. Mr. Dolan remembers Wanda from junior high when she accompanied the orchestra. Mr. Chard said it's fine for us to keep it for now, if we take good care of it. He's hoping you'll learn to play it for the junior high school orchestra."

"Let's take it to Jerry's shop and have him clean it up," said Mae.

The family pulled up to Jerry Cherry's violin shop on Dale Avenue in Richmond Heights. As Tommy lugged the huge instrument into the relatively small shop, he was amazed at the myriad of odd stringed instrument parts crammed into practically every inch of surrounding floor and shelf space. "Well hey there, Tommy," Jerry briefly glanced up as he heard the front door open. He skillfully balanced the bass bridge under the strings in one hand and turned the tuning pegs in the other, as he held a flashlight between his teeth. "How goes it?"

"My brother just brought this home from the high school. Can you take a look at it for us?"

Jerry carefully laid down his tools, wiped his hands and lifted his magnifying glasses to the top of his head before walking over. "Why, of course — let's see what you've got there. By the way — have you met my son Steve?"

Steve Cherry was a couple of years younger than Tommy, and was pounding away on a small drum set in the corner.

"Not bad, Stevie. Not bad," his dad critiqued. "Remember — hold onto the beat. No need to push it. Ya just gotta lay it down, Stevie."

He thought a moment. "You know, if you can find Wanda Lou there a nice set of vibraphones, and teach her a few songs to sing — y'all can form a little combo and get some gigs around town. Maybe my friend Jim can help you out with some vibes." Jim Bolen, a skilled vibraphone and piano player, was also a local TV children's cartoon show host for Cooky and the Captain and the S. S. Popeye.

Ray was able to find an acoustic bass amp, a Fender Rhodes electric piano, and a vocal mic. In a few days the newly-formed Ray Kennedy Trio, along with Wanda, began rehearsing together at the Kennedy house, 7320 Vine Street.

Ray Jr. didn't want to waste precious time. "Give me the list of songs you want to do, Wanda. I'll tell you which ones are good." Ray had a great ear, and when decisions had to be made, Ray let everybody know in no uncertain terms who was boss.

Tommy and Stevie would often clown around or butt heads during rehearsals, and that would make Ray Jr. furious. Wanda occasionally put her foot down. She'd say, "Okay, you guys — I'm giving up too much piano practice time for this. Either get out of the room or let's get down to business."

Ray Jr., Tommy and Steve recorded themselves on cassette tapes. Cassettes were a great tool for recording, listening back and re-recording. Tommy pretended he was a KWMU radio announcer as he introduced the song titles, and then the trio would play.

Mae had no doubt all three of her children would become famous. In spite of their different preferences in musical styles, she hoped they would look for opportunities to perform together. They joined Local 2-197 of the Musician's Union. The trio were interviewed by Regis Philbin, met the comedienne Phyllis Diller, and performed on local TV shows. When the time was right, Mae and Ray arranged for a recording session at Technisonic Studios on Brentwood Boulevard, where Wanda,

Ray Jr, Tommy and Steve Cherry cut their very first 45 record.

Ray and Mae brought the boys to Arthur's on Grand Avenue, and other clubs where the Herb Drury Trio were playing. Herb, Jerry and Art would often give Ray Jr., Tommy and Steve the opportunity to play a set or two. One night, one of the newer managers of the club walked up to Herb and Jerry and said, "I'm not paying for these kids to play - I'm paying *YOU* to play."

Walking toward the band stand, Jerry muttered to Herb, "Hell, I don't care. Let's give the kids some sets *every* time they show up. They're doing great and the audience loves them."

# CHAPTER 18
## Blues, Between and Betwixt *(Stan Kenton)*

### 1971

"Hi there, Harold. Good to see you. How is everything?" Harold Rosenthal had stopped by Kennedy Music.

"Wonderful, Ray. We just had our grand re-opening. I have to admit my wife and I never realized the long hours we'd need to put into a retail store. I sure hope you and Mae make it up there and take a look at the improvements."

Harold had recently purchased Baton Music on Delmar in University City. For many years he had worked as a distributor of brass instruments, and had kept Kennedy Music supplied with a variety of trumpets and trombones.

"Hey Ray — do you remember my son Eddie? He's practicing his trumpet all the time now. Thanks again for the name of that trumpet instructor. Anyway, Eddie is all hopped up on going down to that jazz camp at Drury College in Springfield this summer. Apparently Stan Kenton will be there — you know he's running those jazz clinics all around the country now."

"I did hear something about that, Harold — you know, Ray Jr. and Tommy would probably love to go. Could you send me the literature on it?"

"I've got an application right here, Ray. It's a week-long camp, and to tell you the truth, I'm relieved you might send Ray and Tommy. Let's see — you did say Ray Jr.'s in his teens now?"

"Right."

"So he could keep an eye on the younger two. If you and Mae aren't doing anything Sunday evening, we'd love to have your family over so the boys can all get better acquainted."

The week-long Kenton Camp was an unforgettable experience for the Kennedy boys. Ray Jr. wrote a full-band arrangement, in long-hand, of a new tune he had composed, and submitted it for approval. He was on a different track than Tommy and Eddie, since he had technically had more time with his instrument. Tommy and Eddie had never known so much freedom — the opportunity to live in a college dorm and eat/sleep when they wanted to. The days were intense, and the nights were long.

By the end of the week, Mae couldn't wait to pick up her boys and attend the concert. Mae and Wanda decided to head for Springfield in the morning, and Ray would drive down later.

Mae and Wanda arrived in time to visit with the boys, load the car with their belongings, and help them clean up the dorm room. They entered a dormitory awhirl with noisy middle-school and high school students, some of them blasting away on their instruments, and some of them racing to class. Navigating through the maze of hallways, they found Tommy and Eddie's dorm room. Eddie was neatly packing up his case.

"Hi, Eddie! How was the camp?"

"Man — this camp was a blast, man! We had an amazing week! I've never done so much playing in my whole life. And guess what? They've chosen Buster's original composition for tonight's concert, and he'll be featured on piano! Have you seen Tommy yet?

"No, Eddie — have you?"

"Tommy's been a wild man this week," said Eddie. "He's *REALLY* been digging it. Look — he's right behind you in the hallway —"

Mae and Wanda turned around. They saw a very harried-looking Tommy walking toward them. Mae smiled and reached out her hand to him.

"Hey what's up…" Tommy had a blank look in his eyes. He looked gaunt and his hair looked clumpy. He walked right past his mom and sister, looking for something in the dorm room. He couldn't seem to find it. He turned around to go. "See ya around…"

"What — wait a minute, Tommy…" Mae called out. But he took off down the long hallway.

Mae was worried. She and Wanda walked quickly down the hallway to try to catch up with him. After Tommy turned a corner and vanished, Ray walked by.

"Hi, Mom! I see you found Tommy. I haven't been able to keep track of him. He's acting a little strange."

"Buss," said Mae, "you're supposed to watch out for him. Is he okay?"

"Yeah, probably. But I never see him, Mom. I don't exactly know what his class schedule is, but I do know all the students are gathering tonight in the auditorium at 6:00."

"Well, I'm going to track him down. Do you want to show your sister around?"

Mae walked and walked. She couldn't figure out what the problem was, but she knew something was up with Tommy. Finally, she cornered him.

"I gotta go! I gotta go!" Tommy's eyes looked bleary.

"Tommy, look at me. You're not going anywhere, except with me!" And with that, she grabbed his music case out of his hands and told him to follow her back to the dorm room.

By then, Ray and Wanda had returned to Eddie and Tommy's dorm room.

"Okay, what's going on with Tommy? He's acting like he's lost his mind." Mae was worried.

"Mrs. Kennedy, all I know is that I never see him except when he shows up for class. We hung out together the first couple of days. After that, when I'd run into him, I'd ask him to meet me at lunch time in the cafeteria. He would just say, 'I'll catch you later.'"

"All right, Tommy. I'm taking you to get something to eat. We'll get to the bottom of this."

"See you at the concert, Mom," said Ray.

The cafeteria was closed, so she and Wanda walked Tommy to the car so they could drive into town. They found a diner.

"What do you want, Tommy?"

"Oh, I don't know — okay, I guess I want a turkey plate."

Tommy wolfed down the turkey, dressing, rolls, mashed potatoes and gravy, as if he hadn't had anything to eat for days. He drank two to three glasses of milk. Gradually he began to talk and act like himself again.

"I met this guy named Dave Weckl, who plays a mean set of drums. Dave has been hanging out with Peter Erskine, Kenton's drummer, and we've been staying up all hours. Dave and I have each other's phone

164

numbers — we're definitely going to stay in touch. I'm sorry, Mom — I just didn't feel like sleeping or eating. Sorry I worried you." Tommy sat back in his chair and closed his eyes. "Whew — I need sleep."

Mae found a hotel room nearby. She paid for a quiet room for a few hours, so Tommy could get some sleep before the concert.

That evening, Ray arrived at the campus and met Mae the auditorium just in time. Eddie and Tommy performed in one of the bands, and then Ray performed with his age-level band. After that, the Kenton band played a selection or two. To top the evening off, Stan made this announcement:

"I've asked a few of the students this week to submit a work for the band to play. Right now, let's bring Ray Kennedy Jr. back out here to the piano…"

"Yay Ray…" a group of kids clapped and whistled.

"And he's going to accompany the band on his original composition. He not only wrote this piece — he also arranged it for us."

Kenton turned back around to the band and counted it off. The audience was completely silent throughout the piece, and thunderous applause erupted after.

When everyone was dismissed, Ray Jr. brought a few of the Kenton band members over to introduce them to his parents. "You've got some talented kids here, Ray and Mae. If they keep going the way they've started, we're sure to hear great things from them."

# CHAPTER 19
## Salt Peanuts *(Dizzy Gillespie)*

### 1972

Tommy hesitated to pick up the phone. "Hello?"

"Tommy — you're supposed to be here." Tommy knew she would call. He had hoped no one would notice, at least for a little while. He was supposed to walk directly to the store from school, so that Mae could leave work and prepare dinner for everyone.

"All right, all right. I'm coming up," Tommy responded reluctantly.

Tommy arrived just as his dad and his brother had gotten off the phone with Pat Blunda (Pat's One Stop wholesale record store in downtown St. Louis). Pat had heard Dizzy Gillespie's band was touring again, and was booked for a week in May at the Gourmet Rendezvous in St. Louis. He knew Ray was an avid fan of Dizzy's trumpet playing.

It was getting rather late on a school night during Dizzy's final set, but Mae coaxed Ray afterwards to introduce the kids. Ray had never talked with Dizzy in his life, but he walked up, extended a hand, and exuding confidence he asked whether Dizzy might listen to his older son "play a little something." Dizzy was impressed by the range of color and command Ray Jr. demonstrated at the piano, at such a young age, with *Shadow of Your Smile* by Johnny Mandel. Ray Jr. learned it because it was his father's favorite song at the time. Dizzy asked if he might borrow Ray Jr. the following afternoon.

The next day, a cab pulled up in front of Kennedy Music late afternoon. Mae put dinner money in Ray's pocket, and Ray climbed into the cab with Dizzy. He had the time of his life getting to meet and listen to the band members as they shared their wealth of touring experiences. To the family's surprise, Dizzy and the band worked out an arrangement of *Night in Tunisia* that evening at the Gourmet Rendezvous, which featured a very adept 14-year-old Ray Kennedy Jr. at the piano.

That was a turning point for Ray Jr. His focus from then on was very specific — to move to New York City, where many great jazz artists still lived, and to make his own mark on the world as an accomplished, acclaimed jazz pianist.

# CHAPTER 20

## Will it Go Round in Circles *(Billy Preston)*

### 1974

Throughout childhood and into his teen years, Ray Jr. was rather bossy, especially toward his younger brother, Tommy. Ray Jr.'s usual explanation was that he had way more experience with just about everything, and that Tommy just needed to listen.

Even though Ray Jr. was three years younger than Wanda, Ray normally had the final say in most arguments with her as well. Neither Wanda nor Tommy figured it was worth the time and effort to argue with their brother.

Ray Jr. also tended to worry, a lot like his mother. He even worried *about* his mother — if she appeared to be ill, or seemed overworked, or if maybe just looked at him the wrong way. And if he felt like Tommy was about to cause Mae to lose her temper, he'd find a way to stop him.

Tommy was planning to graduate from Maplewood-Richmond Heights High School in 1978. Chuck, Ray's nephew, had already graduated from MRH back in 1961. Each of them, as they grew up, worked at Kennedy Music. Despite these similarities, Chuck and Tommy grew up in very different decades, and therefore experienced the music store and their Maplewood surroundings in very different ways.

When Tom began attending Maplewood-Richmond Heights High School in the fall of 1974, the school district was struggling financially. Tom found himself rather bored and unchallenged in high school, and he hung around the band and orchestra room as often as he could. When the school day ended, and Tommy was to walk to the music store to go to work, he'd look for excuses to stop along the way to do something — anything else. This, of course, infuriated his brother Ray Jr., and his mother, who depended on him to be on time. But Tommy was bored, and his mind was on his music.

On Fridays, however, Tommy was normally on time for work. In every small business, interesting customers tend to show up. Fridays at Kennedy Music were "Newt days." Ray, Tommy and their cousin, Bob Heimberger (Joe's son) looked forward to seeing Newt. Newt played the harmonica, and he was pretty good at it. But what made him especially interesting to the three teenage boys was that Newt came in *every* Friday and purchased a "Marine Band key of C" harmonica. It was never a different brand, size, shape or key — and so Kennedy Music was sure to keep the harmonica cabinet stocked with plenty of "key of C's," mainly for Newt. Occasionally, just out of curiosity, the boys questioned Newt as to why he wanted or needed yet another key of C harmonica. Didn't he want to try a different harmonica, or maybe another instrument? Newt never explained this odd shopping habit, but he didn't really need to. It was obvious that by the time Newt reached Kennedy Music on Friday evenings, he had already had one too many…and we're not talking harmonicas.

Since Saturdays were busy days at the music store, and since the boys were off school on Saturdays, Mae organized a schedule for them to divide up the day. On Saturdays, another colorful customer often came in -- or, to be more accurate -- dashed in and and right back out. This particular customer purchased a product called Pfanspray, which was a vinyl record cleaner. Pfanspray came in a spray can, with a cleaning cloth attached. The idea was to occasionally spray your records and wipe them down, especially if your record accumulated dust while sitting out on top of the turntable. A little Pfanspray could go a long way. However, and this particular customer would come in and buy two or three cans a week. In fact, he'd sometimes call ahead to be sure there was plenty of Pfanspray in stock. The boys never knew his actual name.

Most of the time, the man would run in, find the Pfanspray, lay his $1.75 on the counter and leave, without any conversation. One day, again just out of curiosity, Tommy asked just before the guy left, "Hey man -- why do you need so many cans of this stuff?"

The man waited a moment or two before responding. Tommy noticed he looked a bit nervous. He paced a bit as he spoke. "I — I just like to take good care of my records. I have some — some real good ones. But sometimes -- sometimes — I just can't find a can of spray."

"Don't you just put the spray can next to your record cabinet?" The conversation peaked Tommy's interest.

The man stood and stared at Tommy blankly for a moment or two before continuing. His voice sounded anxious. "I wish I could do that, — but it's -- hard. Like yesterday — I was just standing in the middle of the room with the can of Pfanspray, minding my own business, spraying my records. But then, weird stuff started happening. The records began to just slip and fly right out of my hands and onto the floor and like — across the room and stuff. The Pfanspray fell out of my fingers, and I still can't find it. I know it's a lot of money, but I really, like, *need* the Pfanspray. Okay?"

One particular Saturday, the Pfanspray customer didn't show up. Tommy was standing in the back of the music store. He was thinking about his life, and feeling sorry for himself that he was being forced to spend yet another boring couple of hours stuck at the music store. It was a Saturday, after all. And why in the world did Wanda get the whole day off? Mom said Wanda had the day off because Wanda was working so hard at college. What kind of lame excuse was that?

Mom and Dad had stepped out on an errand, and Tommy and cousin Bob were alone in the store. Bob was Ray Jr.'s age. Suddenly, Tommy had an idea. Tommy was still under age for a driver's license, but mom and dad had taken only one of the family cars when they had left. The blue Chevy Impala station wagon was still in the back of the store. Ray Jr. wasn't there — and what Ray didn't know wouldn't hurt him.

"Hey Bob," said Tommy, "I'm starving. How about I go get you and me something to eat…"

"Okay, Tommy. Are you thinking about walking down to the Chopsticks House?"

"See ya — be right back." Tommy put his hand in his pocket just after whizzing past his dad's desk and out the door. Bob was curious as to why Tommy had grabbed Uncle Ray's car keys, but he figured Tommy was getting bossed enough by his mom and older brother. He decided to just sit back and let this play out.

Tommy felt a wave of excitement as he steered the huge car in circles, around the big parking lot behind the store. He needed to get the feel of driving. He thought he'd flip on the radio, so he tuned in to KXOK. Judy Collins was singing *Send in the Clowns*, and Tommy began thinking about his boring life again. He pulled out of the parking lot and onto Marshall Avenue. He had to be really careful with the new car, and at the same time he couldn't be away too long. The Dairy Queen in Webster Groves sounded perfect. He used his turn signal and pulled onto Manchester, going west. It was a little tricky, but he only scraped the tires once against the curb as he made the turn.

He stopped at the light at Big Bend — his driving was really okay, he was thinking. The big car seemed to be on the correct side of the yellow line most of the time. He had watched both his brother and his cousin do this lots of times.

The light at Big Bend changed. Tommy saw the Steak 'n Shake up ahead and headed that way. He could just go there and grab some burgers. He *really* wanted those Dairy Queen cheese dogs, though, and besides — anything was better than just standing around and waiting on customers at the music store. Big Bend would have been more direct to Webster, but he would just have to turn left somewhere else. A few feet past the intersection, a huge semi pulled out onto Manchester in front of him. This truck was probably going about 30 mph, but to Tommy it felt more like 10. This drive for a couple of cheese dogs was gonna take forever. Tommy began to worry. He figured Bob wasn't stupid and had to have noticed him taking the car keys. If Tommy left Bob alone in the store too long, would Bob just pick up the phone and blab to Ray Jr., or would he keep quiet?

Was this truck maybe stopping to make a left turn? In Maplewood you could easily get stuck in the left lane behind a turning car. Tommy decided to pull into the right lane, even though technically he knew he shouldn't be passing the truck on the right. He glanced through the rear view mirror — all clear. He gunned it, and to Tommy's surprise, just a few feet ahead of him sat a completely stopped car, preparing to turn right onto Bredell Avenue. He leaned on the horn and applied the brakes.

"Whew, that was close. I almost hit that …"

*CRRRRUNCH…*

"CRAP!"

The huge Chevy wagon's rear-end had fishtailed around to the right as it came to a full stop. How did that telephone pole get there?

Tommy suddenly lost his appetite for the cheesy hot dog. After the rather loud crunching sound, he thought maybe, just maybe, the station wagon was not too bad, based on how it looked from the inside. He couldn't remain stopped where he was for very long, so he got out, pushed the right side of the car off the pole, and maneuvered it back into the driving lane. He made a right onto Bredell and very carefully made his way along the side streets back to the music store parking lot. Tommy breathed a sigh of relief as he walked through the front door of Kennedy Music — no sign of Mom, Dad or Ray Jr.

"Hey Bob — I'd like your advice on something."

Tommy told Bob what happened as the boys walked toward the back parking lot. He had strategically parked next to another car in such a way that the side of the car impacted by the telephone pole wasn't so obvious.

"Yep — we can't just bump *that* dent out, Tommy. You'll need to take Uncle Ray's car to a body shop. You can take it down to Earl Scheib's."

Tommy decided he'd better do that before Ray and Mae got back. Earl Scheib gave him the bad news — $3,000 minimum to repair the '73 Impala. And in 1974, $3,000 in Tommy's mind could have just as well been $3,000,000. He had to come clean.

And when he did, instead of applying for his driver's permit as a sophomore, Tommy had to deal with no driver's license the remainder of his high school years, working at the music store after school, and living under his mother's and older brother's watchful eyes — with the added annoyance of no extra set of car keys left in his dad's desk.

# CHAPTER 21
## Peaches

### 1975

"Whoever came up with a name like that for a record store?" Ray read the ad in the St. Louis Post Dispatch.

Peaches Records and Tapes had come to Hampton Avenue in South St. Louis. Originating in Los Angeles, the chain was advertised as a record and cassette tape Super Center. If Peaches didn't have what you wanted, they would find it — guaranteed. And while you shopped their huge inventory, they also sold concert event tickets for touring country and rock bands.

In spite of this new trend in record retail, Ray and Mae chose to remain a full-service music store. Record and cassette tape sales were a significant portion of Ray and Mae's profits, which they were not prepared to lose to a chain store.

Decade after decade, the Maplewood business district had seen its share of transformations. Once upon a time, foot traffic exiting the streetcars filled both sides of the streets, Manchester and Sutton, all the way from the Maplewood Loop to the City Limits Loop and back again. By 1975 the Maplewood Theatre was no longer operating as a movie theatre. The Brownsom Hotel had already been converted into an apartment building.

After the demise of the streetcar, foot traffic gravitated toward the 7300 block on the south side of Manchester. Only a few businesses remained post-Goldes on the north side of that block — until finally, the brand-new Kmart was complete.

Kmart was accessible through the new parking garage. There were problems with the new garage, however. The give in the upper level of the garage proved to cause undue shakiness. A few new businesses moved into the new storefronts, but the integrity of the garage even caused the floor of the new Kmart store to move. None of the hoped-for new tenants remained in the new storefronts for very long because of this problem.

The biggest problem seemed to be that the municipal garage blocked the view of the new Kmart from pedestrian traffic and others driving along Manchester who were unfamiliar with Maplewood.

Several businesses on the south side of the 7300 block had moved out of the area, or were on the way out, including opticians, attorneys and other professionals with offices on the upper floors. Some of the businesses were no longer relevant (millenary, hosiery and frock shops) while some businesses, like individual grocers and butcher shops, were no longer in vogue. A large boom in the building of suburban shopping malls sent shoppers to Crestwood Plaza and Westroads Shopping Center in Clayton. Some businesses in Maplewood, however, had staying power. Paramount and Laykem Jewelers, Scheidt Hardware, Empire Supply and Kennedy Music were among the businesses that stuck it out through many of the changes.

Ray was now 68, and Mae, 48. Ray's brother, Tom, was about to retire from MacDonnell-Douglass. He came in to chat with Ray from time to time, telling him how carefree he felt.

"Ray," Tom remarked one day, "when you get out from under all of this, we'll take some trips together."

Ray and Mae often dreamed and talked about how they would love to go on an extended vacation to Europe or Mexico. Their short weekend trips to Chicago with Ray Jr., Wanda and Tommy had been opportunities for the kids to hear and meet other performers. Kennedy Music was always closed on Sundays, and so occasionally on a Friday and Saturday they delegated the responsibility of Kennedy Music to a few trusted employees.

Tom continued. "Ray, I'm just sure Mae would prefer you doing the lawn and helping with the house, rather than being tied up here. All wives have some sort of 'honey-do' list. You've worked long and hard — why not talk with the kids to see if they're interested in taking over the music store?"

That was a thought. After Tom left, Ray walked over to Mae as she opened up the mail.

"Even though business seems a little slow these days, it's sure to pick up once those stores across the street are rented. Maybe the music store could be a joint venture with all three of our kids, after their schooling is over. We'll have to have a talk with them. What d'ya think, Mae?"

Mae scanned the letter she held, and then disgustedly slapped it down on the counter in front of Ray. The Kennedys, and Victor Kintz of EJ Drugs, received the same letter from the landlord. As part of the effort to revitalize Maplewood, the building they shared was scheduled to be demolished in two short months.

"Ray — I'm tired."

He had just taken his glasses off for his eyedrops, so he laid the letter down without reading it. "I know — it's been a long day."

Mae's tone became more insistent. "No, Ray — I mean I'm tired of *this*. I'm tired of our weekdays and weekends being tied up with music store planning. The store and school have been wonderful for our family, — don't get me wrong. But I'm tired now of trying to force Tommy or Buster to get up here in the afternoons, just so I can run home and get dinner on the table for us. You know the boys are wanting to move to New York. Wanda is thinking about going for her doctorate, so it isn't fair to place this on her, or on any of the kids if they don't *want* it."

"Don't talk so loudly. One of the teachers in the back might hear you. How do you know the kids don't want it?"

Mae spoke more softly but with the same conviction. "Oh, come on, Ray. You're talking like you have your head in the sand! It's like pulling teeth getting them up here. They're making plans for their careers, and they're performing and preparing for bigger and better things."

"Well, it's still worth a conversation."

178

Mae took a breath and tried a different approach. "Ray, I didn't say anything when you were out a few weeks ago because of your second cataract surgery. But honestly, you have never, *ever* labelled the will call orders legibly as long as I've known you. People come in to pick something up after you've left for the day, and I don't know what to tell them when I can't find it. And you drive Bob, my nephew, crazy with all of the re-counting. You say you've already counted the clarinet reeds and boxes of guitar picks, and then I check the lists against the actual inventory and they're not even close. You're a great salesman, Ray, but to be honest, Bob and I have had to re-do a lot of the work you say you've done — after you leave."

"Aw -- I know your brother Joe must be proud of his son. Bob's a good boy. He just needs to learn my inventory system. Bob is a hard worker."

"Ray, Bob has plans to enroll in the police academy right after high school graduation. Robbie, Hazel's oldest daughter, has been helping out, but she's engaged to be married. And you know your nephew Chuck is happy in his career as a music minister. Every Tuesday night you have a night out, away from the store. And every spare moment I have, I'm trying to keep things in order around here."

"Where are my eye drops?" Ray's right hand shook slightly as he held a tissue and tried to turn the cap of the rewetting solution. Mae offered to help him. She hated to argue with this man. Yes, he was getting older, and his eye issues were becoming a bit of a challenge for the both of them. But Mae knew Ray had always been able to figure out a way to do the things he truly wanted to do. Should she really insist on closing the store? She didn't want to discourage him.

Mae continued, "After you think about this awhile, I think you'll agree with your brother. Remember when Tom Wilson mentioned taking a trip to Tijuana with you? Why, you'll have time to pull out the trumpet

179

and make some music together. One thing I know for sure about you, Ray — you'll *never* stop playing and teaching music. . . nothing gives you more joy."

"Aw, those trumpet-playing days are long gone. . ."

"Will you just listen to yourself? You know you and your musician friends have gotten together over the years when you've had the chance, and you've taught yourself so *many* different instruments."

Mae held Ray's eyes open and helped apply the eyedrops. She leaned forward, gave him a kiss, and spoke a bit more gently. "Ray, I want you to seriously think about this — not for my sake but for your own sake. I promise I won't rush you."

# CHAPTER 22
## Tijuana Taxi (Herb Alpert)

### 1977

In 1975, having had several weeks to make a decision, EJ's Pharmacy relocated one address east, across Marshall Avenue. Kennedy Music decided to move one building west, into the 7310 building. Bob Heimberger, Mae's nephew, along with Ray Jr and Tommy, borrowed Kmart shopping carts from across the street, and made trips up and down the sidewalk, carefully moving smaller fixtures and merchandise from the old location into the freshly-painted new music store.

Mae and Ray were moving into twice the retail space they had had previously, since they no longer wanted the responsibility of instrument lessons and classes.

Wanda built a piano studio with referrals from the music store, at the Kennedy home on Vine Street. She attended Webster University, and earned a Master's Degree in Piano. Her classes prepared her to teach, and her dad instilled in her a love of teaching. Ray was a natural-born teacher. He loved learning various musical instruments, and took great pleasure in demonstrating them to others. Wanda heard more than once Ray's words of wisdom regarding music teaching — "Read the method book and stay at least one step ahead of your student."

Wanda found piano instruction to be fun and rewarding. She also began composing songs. Like her cousin Chuck, she was drawn to church music. She reconsidered the prospect of attending Julliard for several reasons. Her primary reason was that she enjoyed living in Maplewood close to her parents, and that in her musical niche there were plenty of career opportunities in and around the St. Louis area. While her brothers had not yet moved to the Big Apple, Ray Jr. was available to collaborate with her on her first album recording.

Ray Jr. began recording with various artists in and around town. He composed original material and performed at various venues. He gained a following in the jazz world, and was contacted by international jazz artists, recording and performing in places like Stockholm and London.

Tommy was asked to join the St. Louis Youth Symphony his sophomore year of high school, and also the Maplewood Philharmonic Orchestra. He gained regional popularity as a bass player at a very young age. When jazz artists such as James Moody, Barney Kessell, Nat Adderley and Eddie Harris toured the Midwest and needed someone for a recording or for a live gig, they would often call Tommy. He and his brother, Ray Jr., enjoyed serving as clinicians for the Stan Kenton Jazz camps, held at Drury College in Springfield and at various midwestern universities.

Tommy's greatest joy in those days was performing as a jazz duo with his brother, Ray Jr. The two brothers were electrifying on stage — they could anticipate one another's riffs, and their fun was contagious. The brothers would always let their parents know where and when they would be performing together next. Every time they played in St. Louis, individual audience members came up to Ray and Mae and introduced themselves. Ray would jokingly share with them how he had "taught the boys everything they knew." Ray only knew in part how true his words were. Kennedy Music provided Ray Jr. and Tommy, Wanda and Chuck, musical exposure and encouragement — a solid foundation from which they launched lifelong careers.

To Ray and Mae's great delight, one evening in 1976 the old Maplewood Theatre hosted an evening of jazz, featuring Ray Jr. and Tommy, along with their drummer friend Jerry Mazzuca. Many of the boys' school teachers, and classmates attended.

~ ~ ~ ~ ~ ~ ~ ~ ~ ~ ~ ~ ~ ~ ~ ~ ~

Ray finally admitted to Mae she was right — it was time to take that trip to Tijuana, Mexico. He decided to go the summer of 1977 with his friend, Tom Wilson, and brought back lots of pictures. Mae, in turn, took Wanda to Europe to celebrate the completion of her graduate degree. Ray and Mae had four profitable years in their fifth and last music store location. The money was wisely invested, earning inflated yields during the late 1970's — and so their hope of a comfortable retirement appeared more and more attainable.

# CHAPTER 23
## You and I *(Meredith Wilson)*

### 1979

As the very last customer left the building at midnight, Ray's 72-year-old body felt the exhaustion of a 15-hour day. By the end of the night, customers who knew it was an official "Going Out of Business" sale were offering pennies on the dollar for the remaining merchandise. He escorted the last customer toward the front door and locked up.

That's that. Some of the remaining shelving might be useful at home. Mae suggested they hold onto some of the sheet music — *she* might actually find time now to learn to play the piano. Wanda was exhausted too, so they grabbed only their coats and decided to leave all the packing until after the holiday.

In Ray's usual way, he said, "Y'all go on ahead. I'll be right there." Mae knew what this usually meant. He'd be another hour or so getting out the door. She insisted, "Ray, we're exhausted. Let's go now."

But Ray needed to do one more thing. He climbed down the stairs carefully since his eyes weren't the best at nighttime. He felt his way toward the small closet against the back wall. After clearing away a few things, he found the knob and had to pull hard to unstick the door. He reached up above his head through a cobweb to pull the chain on the old light. He peered in, and there near the bottom, propped up on top of an old box and against the back wall was the large, original "Kennedy School of Music" sign. This sign had once hung on the chamfered corner of the old Maplewood Bank Building. Somehow it had survived a small earthquake, a fire, and several moves up and down Manchester Avenue, just like him. He thought about the many clerks, music and dance teachers who had worked alongside him. He thought about Chuck and Peggy, Tom and Mary. He remembered his dad and mom. He thought about the many customers, some of whom had become life-long friends. Most of all, he thought about the day Edith Mae — the love of his life — had stepped off that streetcar so many years ago at the wrong stop, trudging many blocks through the cold just to meet him for a grilled cheese sandwich. "Goodbye, old friend," he said to the sign, as he began to push the old closet door closed again. "I don't think I'll be taking you home with me."

Suddenly, another object a little higher up caught his eye, so he jerked the creaky door open again. He reached up and grabbed his old *KENNEDY'S* music case — the one he had stenciled the lettering on himself as a very young man, and had brought with him on his first summer band trip. The leather handle still felt solid. "This I'll keep."

Ray once again locked the front door and climbed into the car. "Wow, Dad. Where did you get that?" Wanda didn't remember ever seeing the case before.

Ray chuckled. "Aw, this ol' thing? I'll have to tell you about it sometime. Let's go home, Mae."

Mae drove the station wagon back home at the start a new day — Christmas Day, 1979. Wanda helped her dad up the stairs. Her brothers would most likely stroll into the house about an hour or so after their gig, but nobody had the energy to wait up for them. "Goodnight, Mom and Dad." Wanda fell into bed.

Ray and Mae were too tired to say very much as they turned the bed covers down. They took just a moment to sit down next to each other, yawning and stretching. They realized there was no need to set the alarm clock. It felt strange.

Mae yawned and spoke first. "How are you doing, Heathcliff?"

"Hmm — I guess I'll know the answer to that sometime tomorrow. I do kinda like that idea of a cross-country camper trip with Hazel and her husband. We might want to take a few of those old 78 records along, in case we run into a collector on the road." He yawned. "Anyway, I gotta get some sleep now. Merry Christmas, my little Geranium!" He pulled her in gently and gave her a kiss.

"Merry Christmas, Heathcliff — and happy birthday, too!"

"You remembered."

"Breakfast served downstairs at 9:30 am. See you then — bright and early!"

## YOU AND I

*The song You and I by Meredith Wilson was recorded by Will Bradley and his Orchestra, Benny Carter, Ray Charles, Bing Crosby, Tommy Dorsey and his Orchestra featuring Frank Sinatra, Duke Ellington and his Orchestra, Glenn Miller and his Orchestra, the Savoy Hotel Orphans, Dinah Shore and Maxine Sullivan.*

*Ray Kennedy also made a trumpet/vocal recording of You and I. It was made inside a record booth, along with several other recordings with Mae, sometime in the mid 1940's. They were diligent in protecting them since there was no technology available to duplicate them.*

*Today, with the ability to convert audio into digital format, I have been literally listening to my parents' voices as I write this book.*

*Thanks for the records, Mom and Dad.*

## POSTSCRIPT

Every Christmas Eve, after the final closing of the Kennedy Music, Ray was serenaded by his neighbors with the *Happy Birthday* song. One of his trumpet students, who lived at the southeast corner of Vine Street and Marshall Avenue, would ring the doorbell and lead the birthday surprise with his trumpet. Ray enjoyed several more years of collecting and selling musical memorabilia, along with his brother Tom, at area markets.

Immediately after Ray passed away in 1996, Mae sold their house on Vine Street in Maplewood. She continued to enjoy singing and playing her piano, painting individual family portraits, and sharing with her children and grandchildren her love of music, and her many memories of Kennedy Music. She passed away in 2004.

Tom, from the day Mary gave him his first camera, pursued his life-long love of photography, which he shared with his son, Chuck. Most of the photographs included in this book reflect Tom's creative skill with a camera lens.

Hazel, Mae's sister, did not continue her piano studies for very long. She did, however, raise six children and enjoys the company of her 10 grand-children and 5 great-grandchildren. She lives in Arnold, Missouri, and loves to talk about her memories of Kennedy Music.

Chuck and Peggy still enjoy many train rides together — and share their love of music with their children and grandchildren. They currently reside in Texas.

Ray Jr. and Tommy both accomplished their dream of moving to New York City. They have both enjoyed a lifetime of performing their music in many countries. In the jazz world, they are living legends.

Wanda loves teaching piano, playing, directing, leading worship at church, and writing. Maplewood is still Wanda's favorite place to shop, dine and reminisce.

~ ~ ~ ~ ~ ~ ~ ~ ~ ~ ~ ~ ~ ~ ~ ~ ~

To know more about Wanda, Ray or Tommy,
visit their websites:
http://www.wandaspianoarts.com
http://www.raykennedy.com/Ray_Kennedy_Site/Home.html
http://www.tomkennedymusic.com

**Ackowledgements:**

Billboard.com and Downbeat.com

Library and Research Center -- Missouri History Museum

Maplewood Public Library

St. Louis County Library

St. Louis Mercantile Library

Doug Houser

Doug Miner and the 40 South News

Maplewood Merchants, current and past

~ ~ ~

**For additional copies of this book, please contact:**

Wanda Kuntz:  wandaspianoarts@aol.com; 314-440-8208
The Bookhouse: www.BookhouseSTL.com; 314-968-4491